Reflexology
Basics

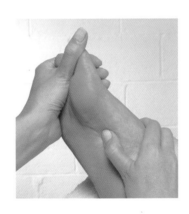

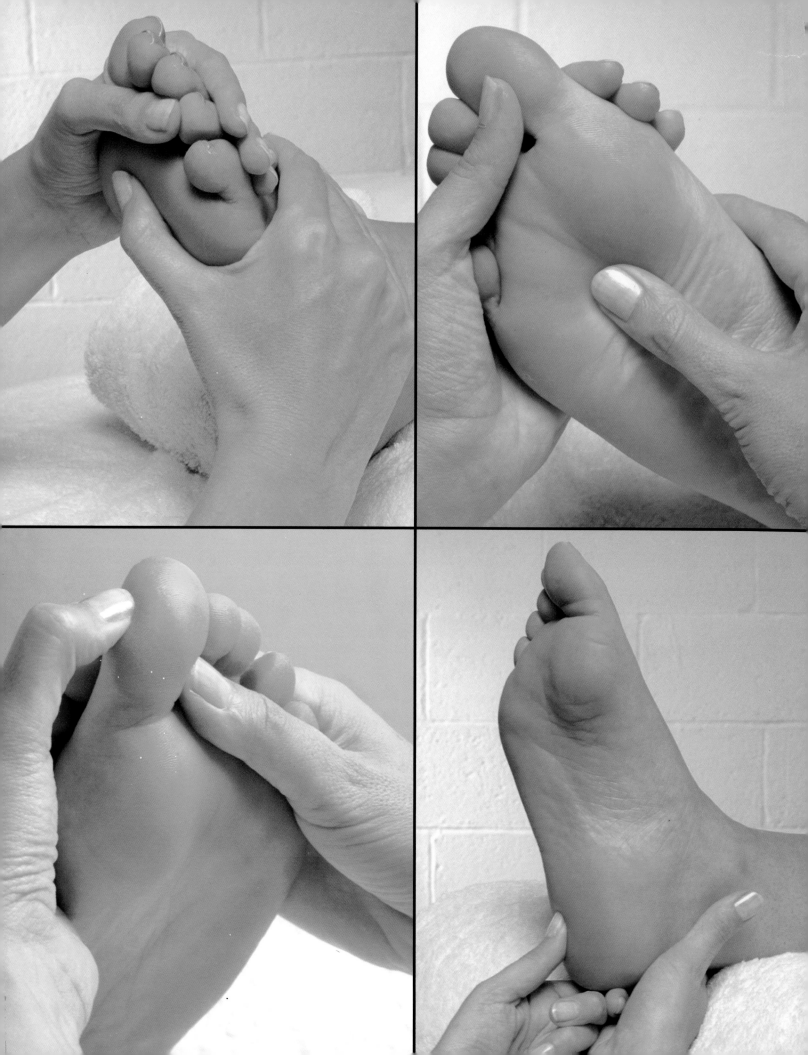

Reflexology

Basics

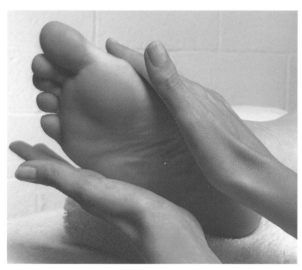

Denise Whichello Brown

BARNES & NOBLE BOOKS

NEW YORK

Library of Congress Cataloging-in-Publication Data Available

2 4 6 8 10 9 7 5 3 1

Published in 2004 by Sterling Publishing Co., Inc.
387 Park Avenue South, New York, NY 10016

Distributed in Canada by Sterling Publishing
c/o Canadian Manda Group, 165 Dufferin Street
Toronto, Ontario, Canada M6K 3H6

Every effort has been made to ensure that all the information in this book is accurate. However, due to differing conditions, tools, and individual skills, the publisher cannot be responsible for any injuries, losses, and other damages which may result from the use of the information in this book.

Editorial Director: Sarah King
Editor: Sarah Harris
Project Editor: Clare Haworth-Maden
Photographer: Paul Forrester
Designer: Axis Design Editions Limited

ISBN 0-7607-6767-X

CONTENTS

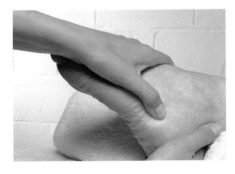

Introduction

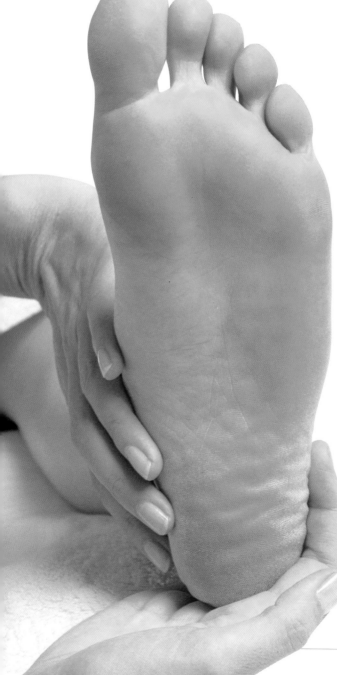

This book is an easy to follow, step-by-step guide to the ancient and gentle healing art of reflexology. The clear illustrations and simple instructions enable the complete beginner to perform a reflexology treatment and to deal with a whole host of common ailments.

Reflexology is natural, noninvasive, easy to perform and remarkably effective. It is also completely safe, provided that it is used correctly, and can be administered to anyone, from young babies to older people. You will need no special or expensive equipment - just a pair of feet to work on! Do not worry if your initial attempts feel clumsy or slow. As you practice, your confidence will grow, and, with experience, you will be able to develop your own unique approach.

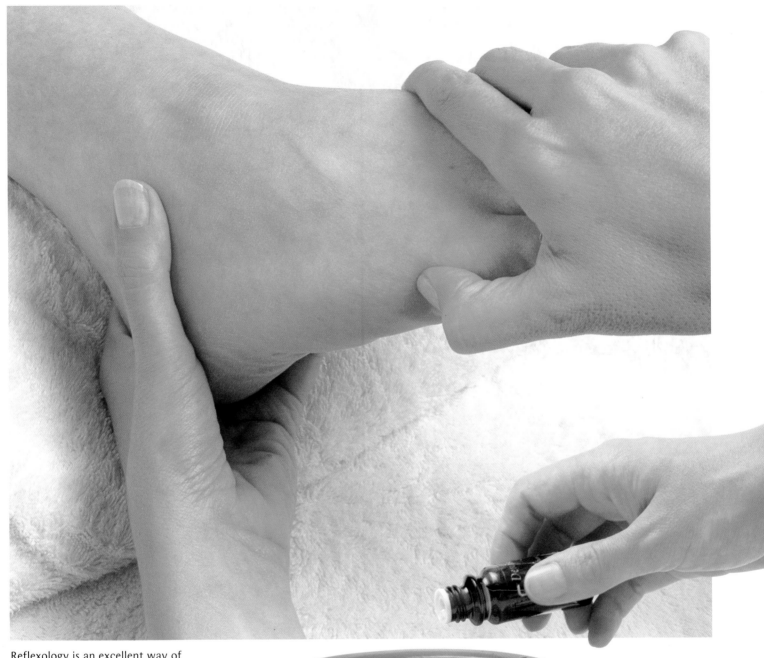

Reflexology is an excellent way of preventing and relieving problems and ailments in all parts of the body. Here work is being carried out on the joints of the body.

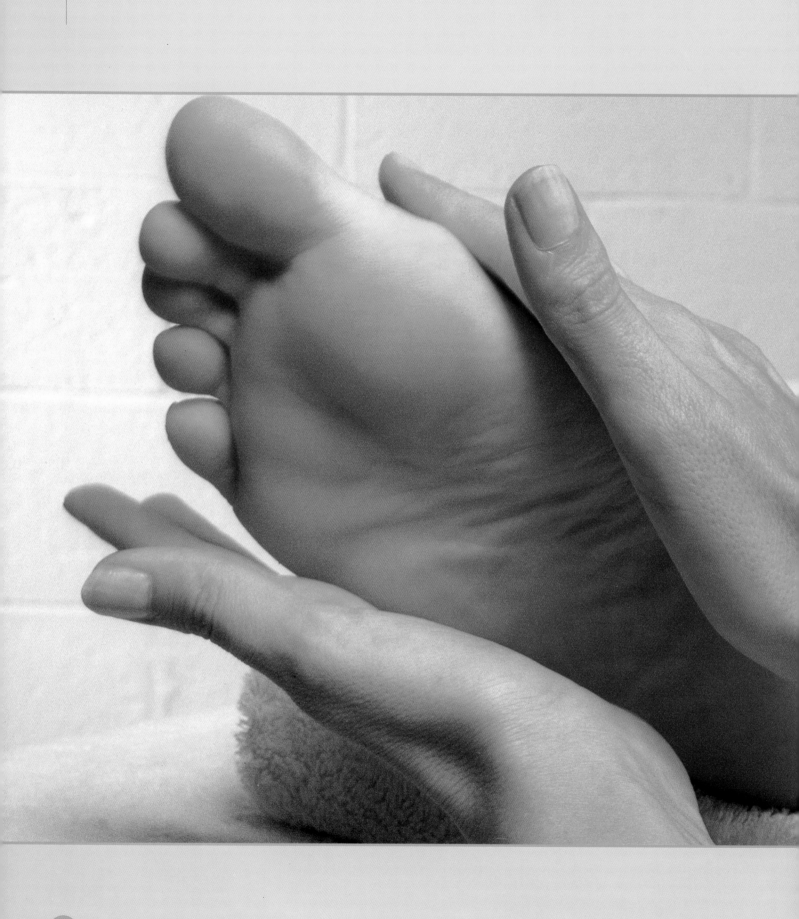

Chapter 1

THE BENEFITS AND THEORY OF REFLEXOLOGY

What is Reflexology?

Reflexology involves the application of gentle pressure to reflex points located on all parts of the feet. These points relate to the internal organs, glands, and structures of the body. The feet reflect, and are a mirror of, the body. Pressure on reflex points can therefore affect and normalize the functioning of the body. The body's natural ability to heal itself is stimulated and health is restored. Everyone can enjoy the benefits that reflexology offers.

REFLEXOLOGY

- induces a deep sense of relaxation

- relieves stress and tension

- encourages the body to heal itself

- improves circulation

- balances blood pressure

- creates an incredible feeling of well-being

- gives more confidence

- deepens sleep and reduces insomnia

- eases aches and pains by relaxing the musculature

- improves the mobility of joints

- detoxifies and cleanses the body of impurities and toxins

- balances the hormones, helping disorders such as P.M.T. and the menopause

- improves the condition and tone of the skin

- relieves indigestion, constipation, diarrhea, and other digestive disorders

- slows and deepens breathing

- encourages the expulsion of mucus

- helps urinary problems such as cystitis

- prevents illnesses from occurring

- stimulates mental function and helps concentration

- seeks out the cause of an illness

- adjusts emotional imbalances

- calms overactivity or stimulates under-activity in any part of the body

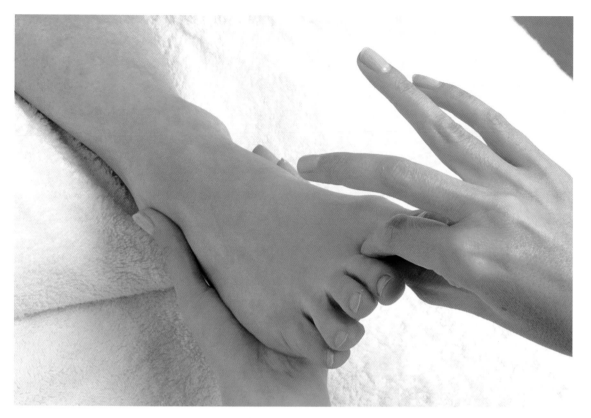

Reflexology helps to detoxify and cleanse the body and aids the fight against infection. Treatment of the point shown will help the upper lymphatics to drain the head and neck area.

CAUTIONS

1. Reflexology is *not* a diagnostic tool. Any diagnosis should be carried out by a medically qualified doctor only.

2. Reflexology should *not* be used instead of orthodox medicine. Medications should never be withdrawn. Reflexology and orthodox medicine complement each other.

3. Although most health problems can be successfully treated with reflexology, the advice of a doctor should be sought if they persist.

4. Reflexology does not claim to "cure" diseases and should never be used to give false hope.

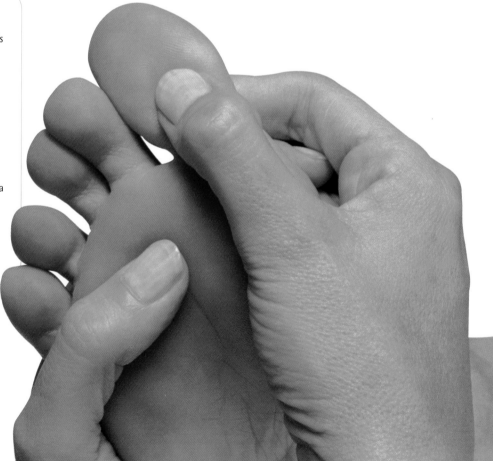

Reflexology on the big toe treats the head and brain area, which will improve mental faculties and ease headaches.

Theory of Reflexology

The Longitudinal Zones

According to reflexology, the body is divided into ten longitudinal zones. If an imaginary line were drawn through the center of the body, there would be five zones to the right of this midline and five zones to the left of it. The zones run the length of the body, from the tips of the toes to the head.

All organs and structures that lie within the same zone are related to each other. Therefore if a reflex point is stimulated in zone one, then the entire zone will be affected.

The right side of the body is represented in the right foot, whereas the left foot reflects the left side of the body. Where we have paired organs, such as the lungs, the right lung will be found in the right foot and the left lung in the left foot. Single organs are found only in one foot. For example, the gallbladder is found only in the right foot, whereas the spleen is located only in the left foot.

Zone One

runs from the big toe, up the leg and center of the body to the head, and then down to the thumb.

Zone Two

runs from the second toe up to the head and down to the index finger.

Zone Three

extends from the third toe up to the head and down the arm to the third finger.

Zone Four

extends from the fourth toe up to the head and down to the fourth finger.

Zone Five

runs from the fifth toe to the head and then down to the fifth finger.

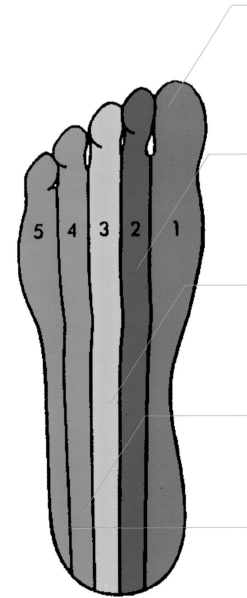

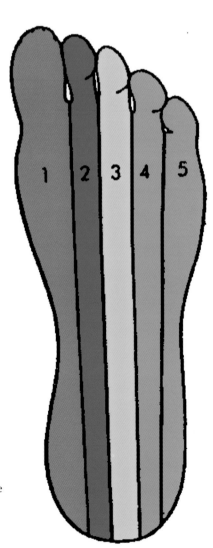

The Four Transverse Zones

Reflexology also divides the feet into transverse, or horizontal, sections, as described below.

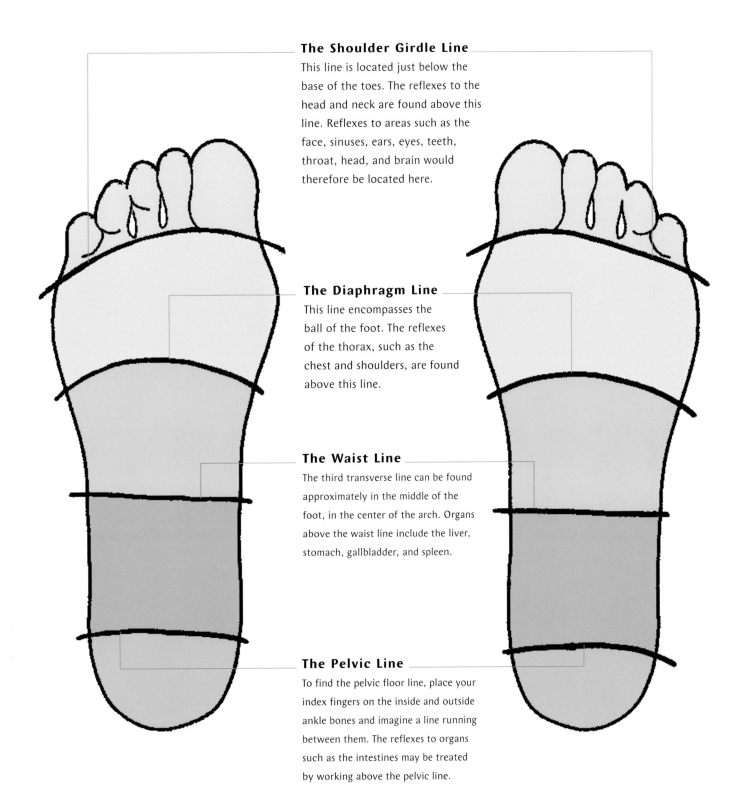

The Shoulder Girdle Line

This line is located just below the base of the toes. The reflexes to the head and neck are found above this line. Reflexes to areas such as the face, sinuses, ears, eyes, teeth, throat, head, and brain would therefore be located here.

The Diaphragm Line

This line encompasses the ball of the foot. The reflexes of the thorax, such as the chest and shoulders, are found above this line.

The Waist Line

The third transverse line can be found approximately in the middle of the foot, in the center of the arch. Organs above the waist line include the liver, stomach, gallbladder, and spleen.

The Pelvic Line

To find the pelvic floor line, place your index fingers on the inside and outside ankle bones and imagine a line running between them. The reflexes to organs such as the intestines may be treated by working above the pelvic line.

Thus it can be seen that the feet really are a mirror image of the body and accurately reflect the whole organism.

Chapter 2

PREPARING
FOR
REFLEXOLOGY

Creating the Ambience

It is essential to create the right atmosphere if the recipient is to derive maximum benefit from the treatment. A few simple steps will help you achieve a calm and soothing environment.

Diffusing essential oils in a burner can also help create a calm ambience, and different oils can be used to help the healing process.

First create a peaceful environment. Take the telephone off the hook so that you will not be distracted. If necessary, tell your family that you are carrying out a treatment and ask not to be disturbed. Place a note on the door to prevent intrusions.

Play some relaxing music. New Age music and Gregorian chants are most therapeutic. Some people find dolphin and whale music very healing. Others prefer such sounds as the wind, sea, and waterfalls, but it is entirely up to the individual. Some people will enjoy silence. Music will ensure that conversation is kept to a minimum and will encourage the recipient to lie back and enjoy the treatment. The more relaxed they are, the more benefit they will derive from the treatment. If the recipient is talking about unpleasant incidents, this may cause undesirable physical reactions in the body, such as muscular contraction of the shoulders. Minimal conversation also enables the giver to concentrate and focus fully on the treatment. Any areas that are out of balance will be more easily detected.

Warm the room prior to the treatment to encourage relaxation. Although it is only necessary to remove shoes and socks to receive reflexology, it is surprising how quickly the body loses heat as the treatment progresses. The body should be covered during the treatment to retain the heat, so have a good supply of towels or blankets at your disposal.

A dimmer switch is a good way of creating subdued lighting. As an alternative light source, use some candles or tinted lightbulbs. Pastel colors, such as pink and lavender, are particularly soothing.

Essential oils are an invaluable way of creating the right ambience and accelerating the healing processes. A small, inexpensive clay burner for diffusing essential oils is ideal.

SOME SUGGESTED OILS:

- frankincense – to heighten awareness
- bergamot – to sedate, yet uplift
- lavender – to relax deeply
- jasmine – to boost confidence
- juniper – to assist detoxification
- cypress – to encourage change
- camomile – to dispel anger and frustration
- clary sage – to create a sense of euphoria
- geranium – to balance the emotions

Positioning the Receiver

The receiver should lie down in a comfortable, relaxed position. This may be achieved in a number of ways. A bed, reclining chair, or sunlounger may be used. You may prefer to work on the floor, using a firm, yet well-padded, surface, which you can make by placing a thick comforter or several blankets on the floor.

A professional reflexologist will use a massage couch. If you become very proficient in reflexology, and are inundated with people requiring treatment, you may decide to invest in one later on.

You will need several pillows for your treatment. Place one or two pillows under the receiver's head, so that you can observe their facial expressions for any reactions. A pillow should also be placed under the knees to take the pressure off the lower back. If the receiver has a back problem, two pillows may be required. A small, rolled-up towel is often placed under the foot that is being treated.

As the receiver lies down, cover their body with a towel or a warm blanket, depending on the temperature. Make sure that they are lying straight, with their arms relaxed at their sides, preferably with the palms facing upward. If their fists are clenched, the energy will not be able to flow freely and tension will be held within the body. Check that the receiver is not wearing any restrictive clothing: belts, neckties, or tight clothes should be loosened to maximize the receiver's comfort.

You will need to place a swivel chair or stool within easy reach of the receiver's feet. It is important that you are comfortable so that your own energies are not impeded. If you are in an uncomfortable position, your tension will be communicated to the receiver. You will also find it difficult to enjoy giving the treatment and will find it hard to detect any reflexes requiring attention.

To relieve pressure on the lower back, a pillow should be placed under the receiver's knees. Two may be required should the receiver suffer from back problems.

PERSONAL PREPARATION

- take off all jewelry to avoid scratching the receiver
- wear comfortable, loose-fitting clothes – you need to be able to move around freely and to relax
- trim your nails closely to avoid them digging into the receiver; make sure that they are scrupulously clean
- do not wear strong perfume, as this can be very off-putting if the receiver does not like the smell
- consciously relax yourself prior to the treatment: close your eyes, take a few deep breaths, and, as you breathe out, let go of all your tension and feel your neck and shoulders relax

For ease of treatment, the foot should be raised. A small, rolled-up towel placed under the foot is ideal.

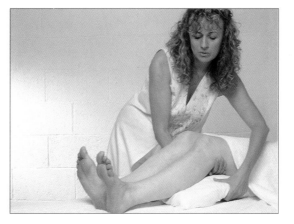

One, or preferably two, pillows should be placed under the receiver's head. As well as providing more comfort, this will allow you to see whether their reaction is reflected in their expression.

Physical Examination

Visual examination of the feet can supply you with lots of important information. The feet have many stories to tell. A "perfect" pair of healthy feet will be pink, unblemished, and pleasantly warm. They will also be relaxed and supple. Unfortunately, such feet are very rare.

POINTS TO LOOK FOR:

- bunions
- toe deformities
- flat feet
- veruccae
- athlete's foot
- hard skin
- dry, flaky skin
- cracks and crevices
- scars
- cuts
- color – pink, white, red, purple
- swelling
- abnormalities of the nails
- temperature
- odour
- chilblains
- pigmentation
- lumps

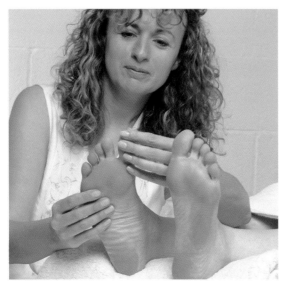

As you observe the feet, remember that the type of any abnormality is not important. It is the *site* of the abnormality that indicates where the energy flow is disrupted.

On one occasion I noticed a very small scar over the uterus area of a patient's foot. Interestingly, she was unaware of this scar, but was prone to miscarriages. Asthmatics will often have hard skin or small lumps over the lung area. Irritable-bowel syndrome (I.B.S.) will show up in the foot as a lack of tone in the reflex area of the colon. A heavy smoker will often have very yellow skin over the lung area. Individuals with bunions may suffer from neck problems. Tiredness and exhaustion will often result in white feet, while anger and frustration may turn the feet red. During periods of change, the skin on the feet may sometimes peel off, as the body lets go of the past and prepares for the new. The feet reveal all.

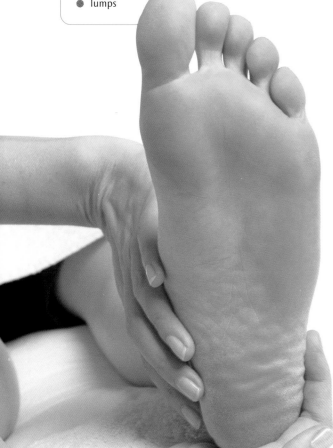

EXERCISE CAUTION

- Use gentle pressure over the pancreas area when treating a diabetic. Use less pressure than normal, as the skin can be thinner and bruise more easily, while diabetics have a slower healing rate. In severe cases of diabetes, the treatment time should be reduced to 20 minutes.
- Corns, calluses, and bunions: use only gentle pressure, especially if they are tender.
- Heart problems: avoid the heart area if a pacemaker has been fitted, and take care if the receiver has cardiac problems.
- Epilepsy: take extreme care over the head and brain areas.
- Use gentle pressure over varicose-vein areas and exert extremely gentle pressure if the receiver has osteoporosis, due to the fragility of their bones.
- If the receiver has a verucca or athlete's foot, avoid the affected areas and treat those areas on the hand instead.
- When treating children, a much lighter pressure is required. A short treatment, not exceeding 10 to 15 minutes, should suffice.
- Take care and be very gentle with terminally ill receivers. Reflexology can be very beneficial in these cases, as it improves elimination, relaxes, and provides pain relief.
- Use lighter and shorter treatments for older receivers whose skin is fragile.

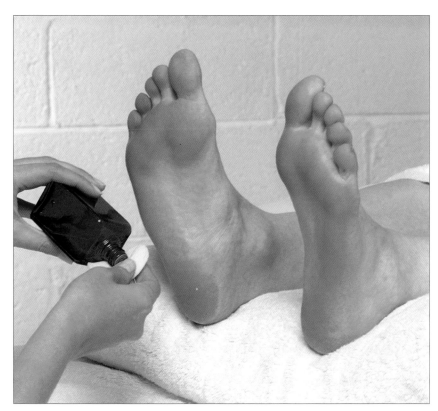

Rose water is an excellent choice for refreshing and cleansing the feet.

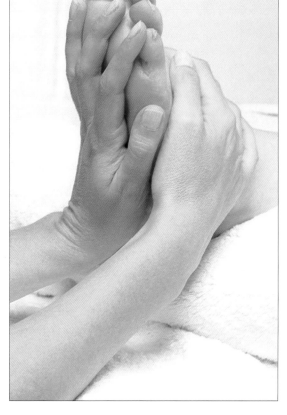

Refreshing the Feet

Prior to a treatment, you may wish to refresh the receiver's feet. Do *not* do this before your physical examination, however, as much valuable information could thereby be lost.

You could provide a bowl of water for the receiver to soak their feet in if they have been standing up all day. In the summer, a bowl of cool water containing a few drops of essential oil of peppermint or lavender is very refreshing. Alternatively, you could add a sprig of fresh lavender or mint to the water. A few drops of essential oil of lemon, or the juice of half a lemon, is very refreshing. Tea-tree oil is becoming very popular and is an excellent addition where there is a fungal infection, such as athlete's foot. A bowl of warm water containing a few drops of essential oils of ginger, rosemary, or black pepper is warming in the winter. A footbath is also a relaxing and refreshing treat for feet.

Rose water is beautifully perfumed and excellent for cleansing the feet. It is also far less messy than a foot bowl. Use a fresh piece of absorbent cotton for each foot, in case there is any infection: you would not want to spread an infection from one foot to the other.

Ensure that you do not use too much pressure when treating the feet. The receiver will let you know if you are pressing too hard.

CONTRAINDICATIONS AND CAUTIONS

Although reflexology is a very safe therapy when performed correctly, there are some occasions when treatment is inadvisable or care should be taken.

WHEN TREATMENT IS INADVISABLE OR NEEDS A DOCTOR'S PERMISSION

- In the case of any serious condition that is being treated by a medically qualified practitioner, their consent should be obtained. Reflexology is usually acceptable.
- Fever: wait until it has subsided. As the body is already fighting off toxins, a reflexology treatment would release more unwelcome toxins into the system.
- In a case of deep-vein thrombosis and phlebitis, the clot could move, resulting in a fatality.
- Immediately after surgery, due to the risk of thrombosis. Research shows that reflexology can accelerate recovery times, but only short, light treatments should be given.
- If the recipient has a contagious skin condition, such as scabies, impetigo, ringworm, measles, and mumps.
- During pregnancy, where there is an element of risk, especially during the first 16 weeks if there is a history of miscarriage.
- Never press directly on cuts, bruises, recent scars, or severe varicose veins.

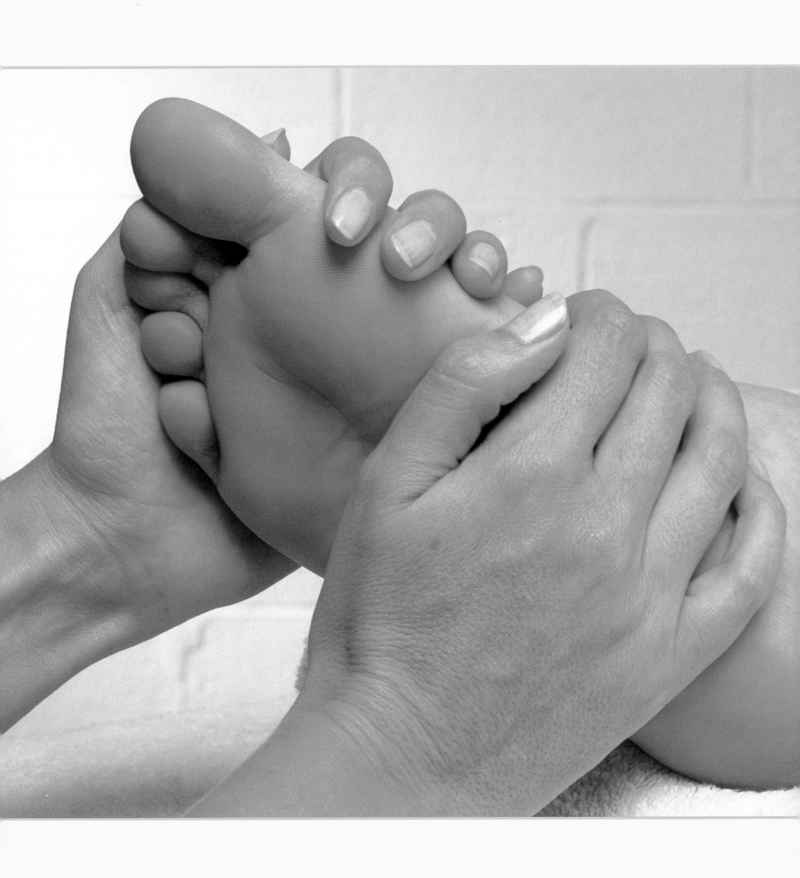

CHAPTER 3

THE WARM-UP

THE WARM-UP

Relaxation techniques should always be used prior to, and at the end of, a reflexology session. At the beginning of a treatment, they help to build up a relationship of trust and to dispel any worries that the receiver may have. Some people tend to be rather nervous when experiencing their first treatment. Not only is it a new experience, but they may worry unduly that they will be ticklish. Yet reflexology never tickles if you pick up the feet with confidence.

These massage techniques are also used during the reflexology routine to soothe and relax and to help to eliminate any toxins that have been released when pressing on the reflex areas.

Relaxation techniques are designed to loosen any tension in the feet, too. They will become supple and flexible and therefore much easier to work on.

Do not use oils or creams during any part of the treatment, as the feet will become too slippery to work on effectively. Save these for a relaxing massage at the end of the treatment.

No oils or creams should be used during the preliminary relaxation sequence, nor should they be used during the treatment. Otherwise the feet will become too oily to work on and it is impossible to work on the reflex points and to feel any sensitive areas. At the end of the treatment, however, it is highly beneficial to massage the feet with cream or oil in order to keep them smooth and moisturized.

The warm-up techniques that I describe may be used in any order. It is not essential to perform all of them. Choose your favorite techniques and create a few of your own.

GREETING THE FOOT

STROKING THE FOOT

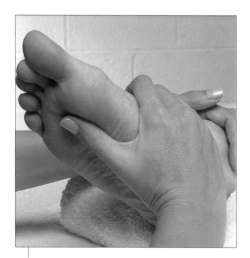

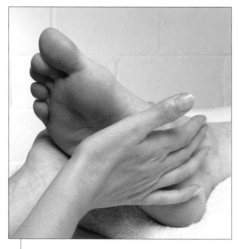

Take hold of the receiver's foot between both of your hands and gently clasp it for about a minute. This initial contact helps to relax and reassure the receiver and also enables you to tune in to them.

1 Using both hands, stroke the whole foot firmly, covering the top, the sides, and the sole of the foot. Work up from the toes, gliding around the anklebones, and return your hands to the starting position with no pressure.

2 Repeat this movement several times. Stroking relaxes, increases the blood flow, and helps to disperse any excess fluid, especially around the ankles.

OPENING THE FOOT

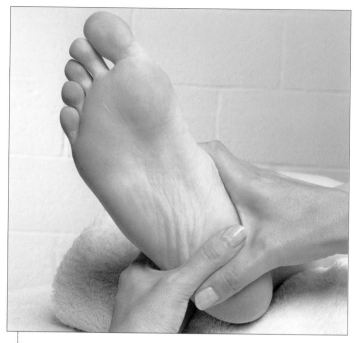

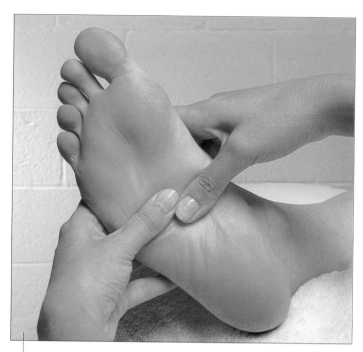

(1) Hold the foot with both hands, so that your thumbs are placed flat against the sole and your fingers are flat on top - one hand will be slightly higher than the other. Pull your thumbs away and past each other toward the edges of the foot and then allow them to slide back toward each other.

(2) Work your thumbs in this zigzag movement from the base of the heels and back again. You will feel that you are opening out the foot.

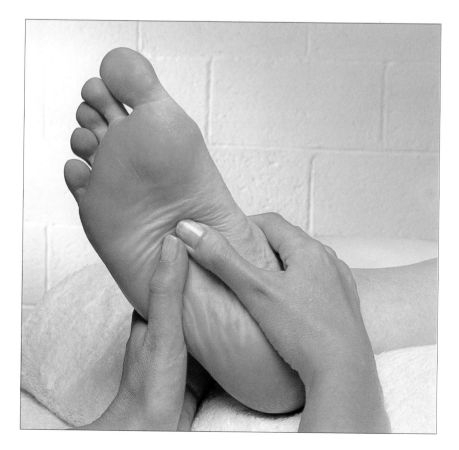

THUMB-SLIDING

Interlock your fingers and place them on the top of the foot. Place both of your thumbs at the base of the heel and slide them up to the top of the foot.

SPINAL-STROKING

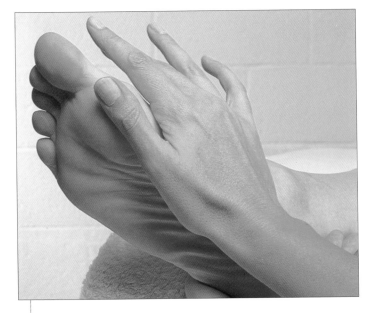

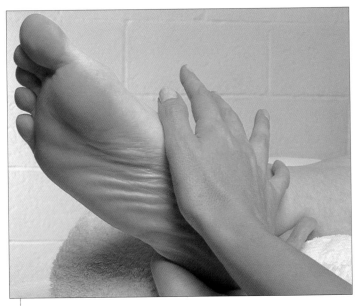

(1) Cup the heel of one foot so that it is resting in the palm of one hand. With the heel of the other hand, stroke firmly down the inside of the foot, working from the big toe toward the heel.

(2) As the inner edge of the foot corresponds to the spine, this technique encourages the spine to relax and is excellent for neck- and back-pain sufferers.

METATARSAL-KNEADING

SPINAL TWIST

FIST-SLIDING

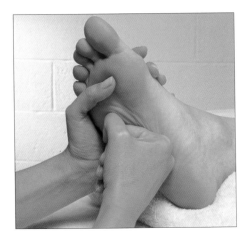

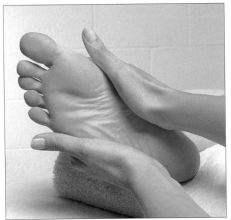

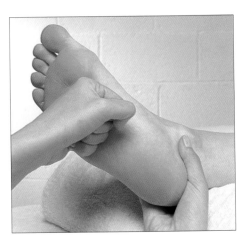

Hold the top of the foot with one hand just below the base of the toes. Your hand should wrap around the foot, with your thumb on the sole and your fingers on the top. Make a fist with your other hand and place it on the fleshy area on the ball of the foot. Work from the ball of the foot to the heel, using a gentle, circular motion. This technique helps to soften the tissues on the sole of the foot.

Place one hand on the inside of the foot and the other on the outside. Using the heels of your hands, pull the outside of the foot toward you with one hand as you push the inside of the foot away from you, and vice versa. Work along the edges of the foot from the heel to the toes and back down again. Perform these movements slowly to further relax and improve mobility in the spine.

Support the foot under the heel with one hand and place the fist of your other hand on the heel area. Slide it slowly from the bottom of the foot to the tips of the toes.

ANKLE ROTATIONS

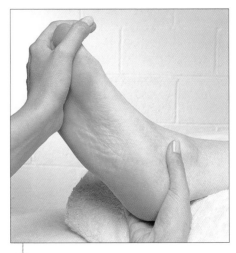

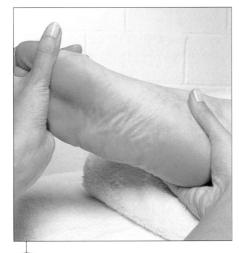

(1) Support the heel in one hand, with the thumb on the outside of the ankle and the fingers on the inside. Grasp the top of the foot with your other hand and then slowly and gently rotate the ankle several times in one direction and then in the other.

(2) This movement helps relaxation and increases mobility in the lower back and pelvis.

FOOT-ROCKING

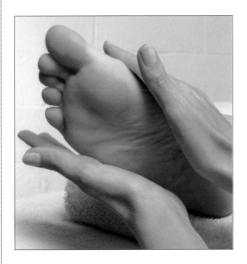

Place the palms of your hands on either side of the foot. Move them alternately and rapidly from side to side, so that the foot vibrates. This movement stimulates circulation and relaxes the muscles in the foot, ankle, and lower leg.

FIVE-TOE ROTATION

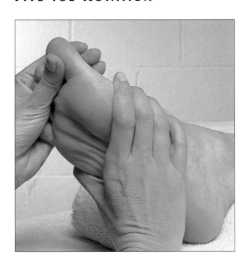

Support the foot in one hand, and, with your working hand, place your thumb on the sole of the foot and your fingers on the top. Rotate all of the toes at once to encourage increased flexibility.

FLICKING

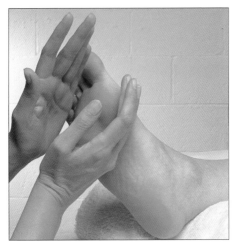

Using the little-finger side of both hands, gently flick them up and down the sole of the foot. This is a very stimulating movement that is useful for energizing.

TOE-LOOSENING

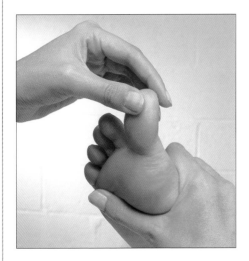

Support the foot gently with one hand, with the thumb on the sole of the foot and the fingers wrapped around the top. Using your other thumb and index finger, gently stretch each toe and then rotate each clockwise and anticlockwise. This will increase the flexibility of the toes and will loosen the neck and reduce mucous in the sinuses.

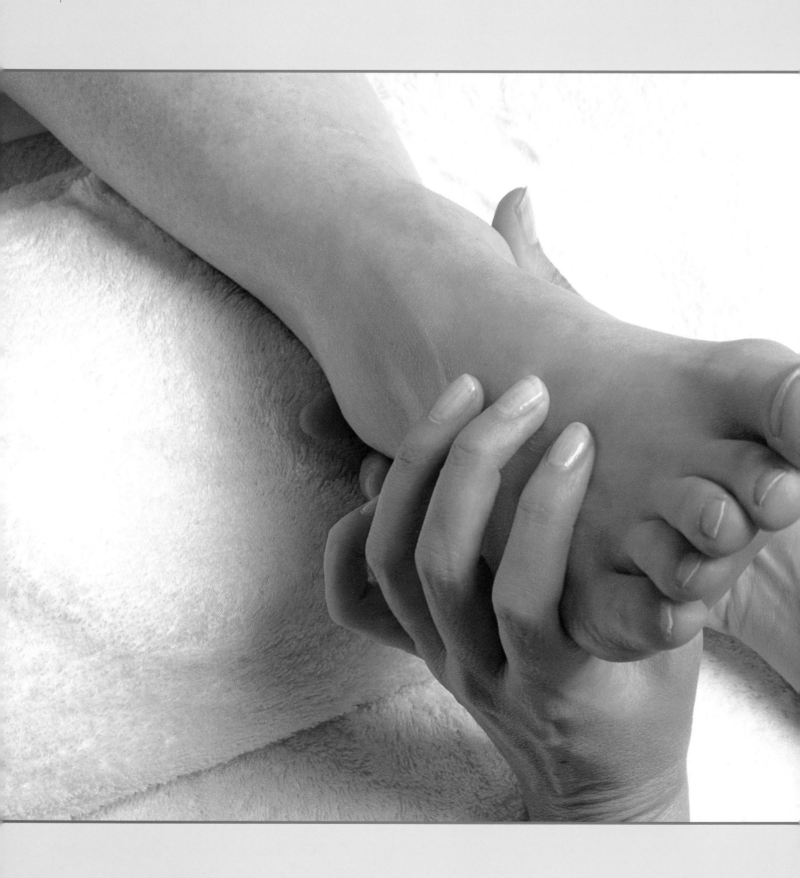

CHAPTER 4

REFLEXOLOGY TREATMENT TECHNIQUES

REFLEXOLOGY TREATMENT TECHNIQUES

Prior to performing a full reflexology treatment, it is important to master, and feel confident with, the basic techniques. In this step-by-step guide, we will be using all of the the techniques described in this chapter.

Before you begin, ensure that your fingernails are scrupulously clean and that they are trimmed down as far as possible. As you apply pressure, even a short nail digging into the skin can be uncomfortable, or even painful, for the receiver. Check that you have removed any watches, bracelets, and rings.

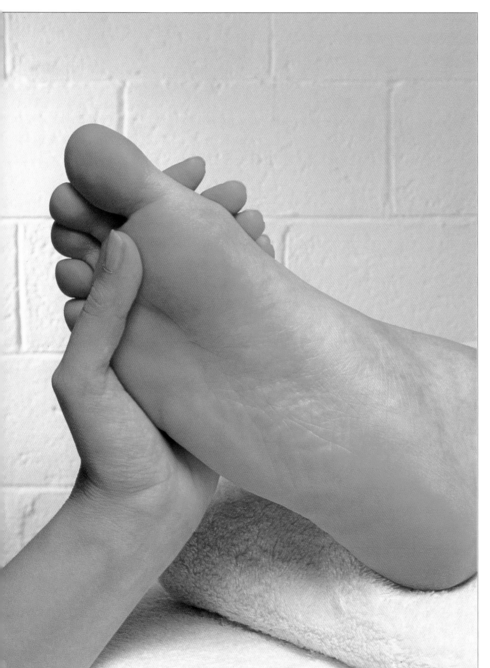

Supporting/Holding Technique

It is vital that you support the receiver's feet properly during the treatment so that you are able to reach, pinpoint, and stimulate the tiny reflex points easily, accurately, and effectively. Gentle, yet firm, support will create a feeling of trust and confidence.

You should always be holding the foot with both hands. One hand is used to support the foot gently, while the other hand works into the reflexes.

Hold for Working Above the Waist line

When working on the upper part of the foot above the waist line, place the heel of your hand against the outer aspect of the foot. Wrap the fingers of your hand lightly over the front of the toes, with your thumb resting gently on the ball of the foot. This foot hold allows you to support and control the foot very effectively. Remember not to grip the foot too lightly, however.

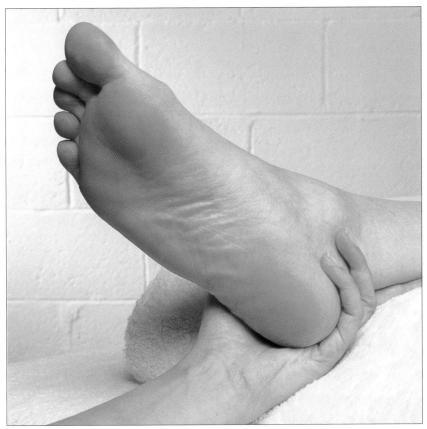

Hold for Working Below the Waist line

If you are working on the lower part of the foot, below the waist line, simply rest the heel in the palm of your supporting hand.

Alternative Holding Technique

You may also support the foot by using the palm ,or the flat of your hand. Your fingers may point upward, toward the toes, or downward, toward the heel. This position is particularly effective when working the inner aspect of the foot.

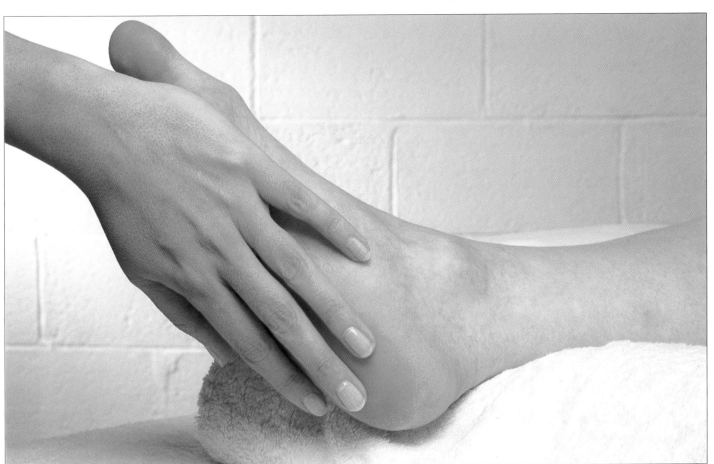

Thumb-walking/Caterpillar-walking Technique

This technique is used for working on a large area of the foot. It is a very relaxing and therapeutic movement. As the name suggests, the thumb literally "walks" over the surface of the area being treated.

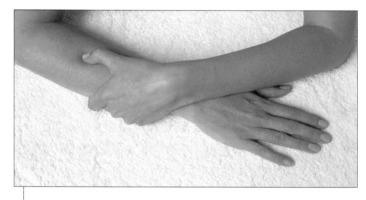

(1) The outer edge of the thumb is used to perform this movement. Place your hand, palm downward, on a table and note that the tip of the thumb touches the surface of the table – this outside tip will be the thumb's working area.

(2) First practice the caterpillar-walking technique on your forearm. To walk the thumb, slightly bend the first joint of the thumb *only* and then unbend the joint a little. Make your thumb take very *small* steps as it "walks" along the hand and forearm.

(3) he walking movement is always performed moving forward – never backward or sideways. You should aim to maintain a constant, steady, and even pressure. An on-off, on-off pressure should not be felt at each bend of the thumb. Do not worry if your thumbs start to ache or feel sore at first. As you practice, your thumbs' tolerance will increase and they will build up strength. Stay patient and keep trying. As the thumb is "walking," the four fingers should be molded to the contours of the hand or forearm. The fingers should be held together comfortably to ensure maximum leverage. If they are spread out, some of the leverage will be lost.

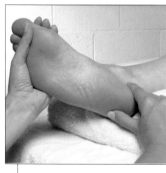

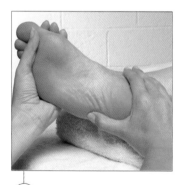

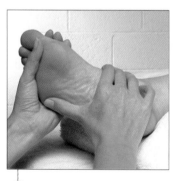

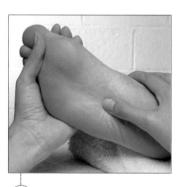

(4) Now practice thumb-walking up each of the five zones along the entire length of the foot. Ensure that you are holding the foot correctly, with your supporting hand wrapped around the toes.

(5) Work upward from the base of the heel in zone five toward the base of the little toe.

(6) Now work upward from the base of the heel in zone four toward toe four. Repeat your thumb-walking up zones three, two, and one.

(7) Finally, thumb-walk up each of the five zones on the other foot.

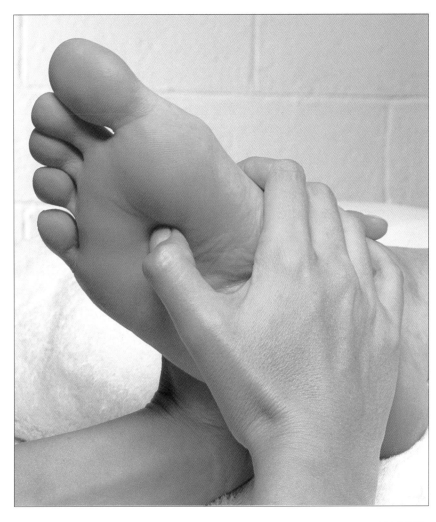

- that you are not digging your nails into the skin

- that you are not gripping the foot too tightly

- that you are using the *outer* edge of your thumb

- that you are bending only the first joint of the thumb slightly, It should neither be too bent nor too straight

- that your "steps" are very small

- that you are using a constant, even, and steady pressure

- that your pressure is firm, but not hard enough to cause the receiver discomfort

- that your thumb only moves *forward*, not backward or sideways

This picture shows that the thumb is too bent to treat the foot effectively.

This illustrates the ideal thumb posture, with only the first joint bent slightly.

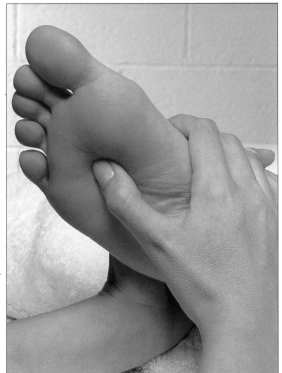

Here the thumb is too straight to carry out an effective treatment.

Finger-walking

The finger-walking technique is basically the same as the thumb-walking technique. Finger-walking is used in preference to thumb-walking on bony or sensitive areas, such as the top of the foot. It is also useful for working around the ankle.

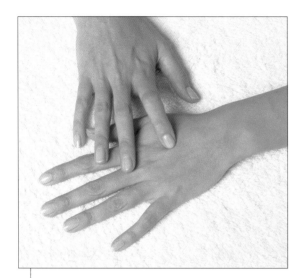

1 Instead of using the first joint of the thumb, the first joint of the index finger is used. Excellent places to practice finger-walking are on the back of your hand or on your forearm. Use the edge of your index finger as you "walk" forward, taking the smallest steps possible while exerting a constant, steady pressure. Leverage is obtained by the use of the thumb in opposition to the fingers.

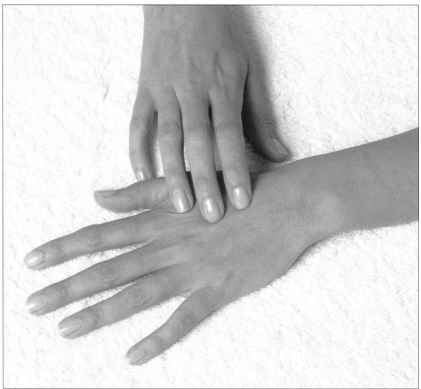

2 Once you have mastered finger-walking with your index finger, try using your other fingers. Any finger or fingers may perform this technique.

3 Now practice the technique on the receiver's foot. Try using one finger at first.

4 Now use two or more fingers to "walk" across the top of the foot.

Hook in and Back up/Pinpointing Technique

This technique is used to apply pressure to specific points that require great accuracy. Certain points on the feet are either too small or too deep for the walking techniques to be used effectively.

The technique is ideal for contacting a tiny reflex point, such as the pituitary gland, which is found on the big toe. You would never use this technique to cover a large area of the foot. The technique has been likened to a bee inserting its sting: a bee lands on your skin and then backs its sting into your flesh. Similarly, your thumb lands on a small point, hooks in and backs up.

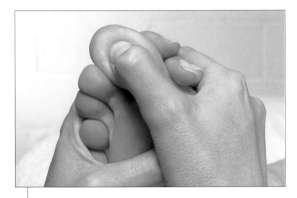

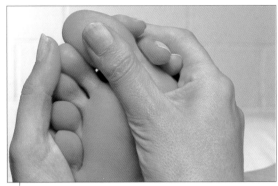

(1) The outside edge of your thumb will be your contact point. Place the thumb of your working hand on your chosen reflex point.

(2) Apply pressure with your thumb to this point. Now pull your thumb back across the point. Push in, then back up. You may repeat this technique several times.

Pressure Circles on a Point

This technique is particularly recommended for working on tender reflexes or sensitive areas of the foot. Pressure circles are usually performed with the pad of the thumb, although occasionally a finger may be used.

Technique Using the Thumb

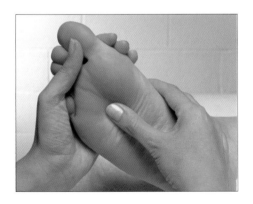

Hold the foot comfortably with one hand and place the flat-pad part of the thumb of the other hand on the tender area. Slowly press into the area and gently circle your thumb over it several times. After a few pressure circles, any tenderness should have diminished.

Technique Using the Finger

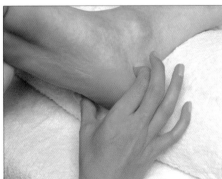

The index or the third finger is used when working on the ovary/testicle or uterus/prostate reflex points. Here the uterus reflex is illustrated.

Rotation on a Point

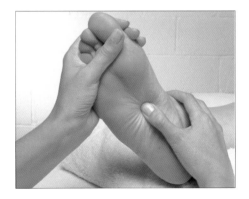

This technique involves pinpointing the area to be treated and rotating the foot around it. Place the pad of your thumb on the reflex point. With your holding hand, gently flex the foot slowly into the thumb. Rotate the foot in a circular motion around the thumb.

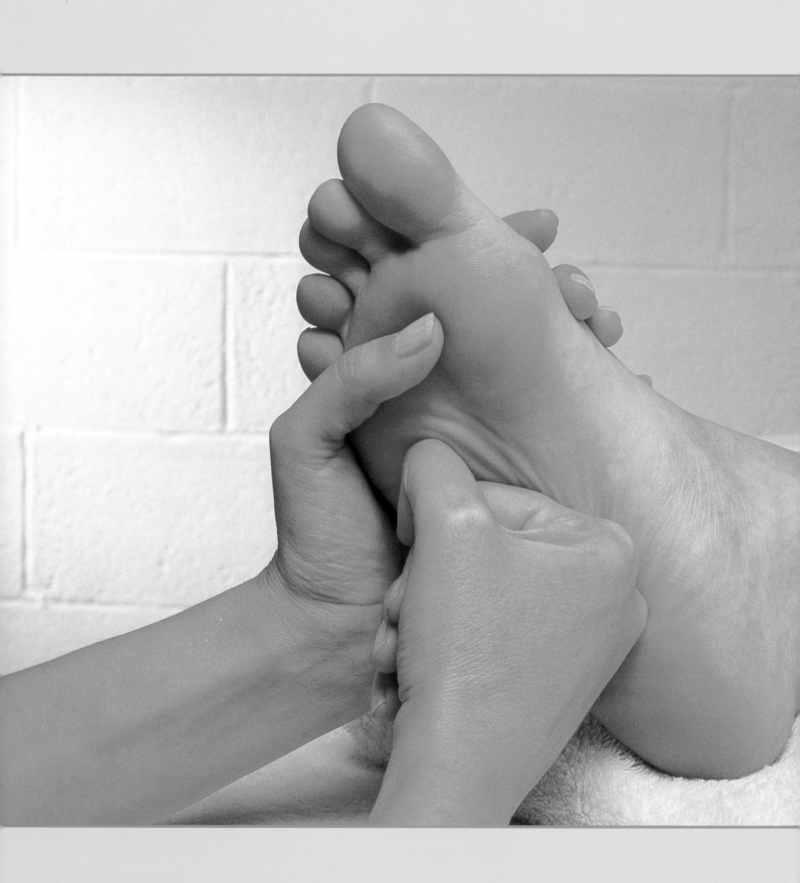

CHAPTER 5

STEP-BY-STEP GUIDE

Step-by-step Guide

This section of the book will guide you step by step through a complete reflexology routine. Color photographs and detailed instructions demonstrate very clearly how to perform the treatment. The entire right foot will be treated before moving on to the left foot. When familiarizing yourself with the sequence, it is very confusing frequently to switch from one foot to the other. There is also the danger of losing contact, which will affect the continuity and flow of the treatment.

Treatment

The length and number of reflexology treatments will vary, depending upon the individual. However, as a general rule, an average treatment (with practice) will probably take you about forty-five minutes. Some of the factors that will need to be taken into consideration are as follows.

The Age of the Receiver

When working on a young child, a short treatment consisting mostly of stroking movements and not exceeding ten to fifteen minutes will suffice. A baby should not be treated for more than five minutes using mostly stroking movements and very gentle pressure with the index finger (not the thumb) on the troublesome areas. Babies and children usually respond very rapidly. If you are working on an older person, a shorter treatment may also be necessary.

The Fitness of the Receiver

If the receiver is very sick, or even terminally ill, the treatment again needs to be shorter. Do not be afraid of working on terminally ill people – I can assure you that it can be very rewarding. Reflexology can offer pain relief and a wonderful feeling of well-being and deep relaxation. It also helps to improve the function of the bowels, which can become sluggish due to the drugs that usually have to be administered.

Diabetics will also often require a shorter treatment time, particularly in severe cases. The skin is inclined to be thinner, bruises easily, is more prone to infection, and heals more slowly. The treatment time may be reduced to twenty minutes.

Sensitivity to the Treatment

If a client has very sensitive feet and reacts strongly to the treatment, then the treatment time will need to be reduced. This may occur if a person is extremely anxious or is going through an emotional trauma.

It is very important that you use your intuition, as well as your common sense. Do not assume that the longer the treatment lasts, the more effective it will be. If a session is too

lengthy, you could overstimulate the body.

As regards frequency of treatments, for optimum results, carry out the complete reflexology routine for six to eight treatments.

After the initial sessions, a treatment is recommended once a month to help to maintain the receiver's health and to prevent problems from reoccurring.

You should *not* perform a *complete* treatment every day, as the body needs time for self-healing between treatments. As we work on the feet, we stimulate the body's natural healing forces and must subsequently allow them to do their work.

POSSIBLE REACTIONS DURING A TREATMENT

- changes in expression: for example, a frown could indicate a slightly sensitive area
- audible noises, such as laughing, sighing, and crying
- visible contraction of the muscles – in the shoulders, for example
- gestures of pain: a sharp pain usually indicates an acute problem; a dull pain indicates a chronic problem
- a feeling of deep relaxation and the desire to sleep
- a warm glow as energy blockages are released
- feelings of euphoria
- sensations of the body expanding and spreading as it relaxes
- a running nose if the head zones are being treated and are blocked
- twitching or tingling
- warmth in the area of the body being worked on
- excessive perspiration

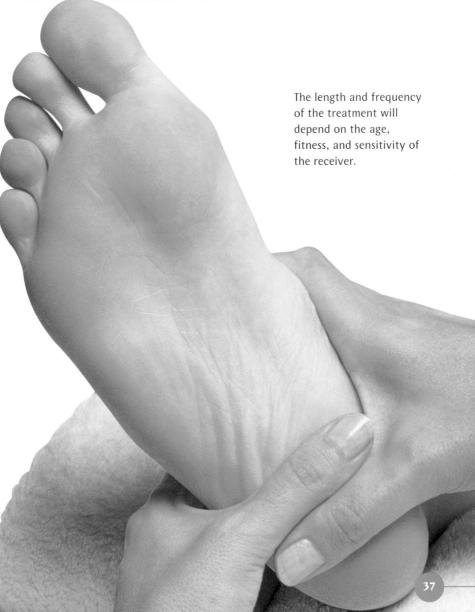

The length and frequency of the treatment will depend on the age, fitness, and sensitivity of the receiver.

Reactions to Treatment

During and between treatments, both physiological and psychological changes may occur. All responses should be seen as highly positive and as demonstrating that your treatment is really working. Some form of reaction is inevitable as the body tries to rid itself of toxins. Since the reactions are related to cleansing, many tend to manifest themselves in the organs of elimination, for example, the bowels, kidneys, and skin. As you read through the lists that follow, do not panic. During or after a treatment only one or two reactions may occur, and, if they do, they are usually short lived and should disappear within twenty-four hours.

What to Do if the Receiver Experiences a Strong Reaction

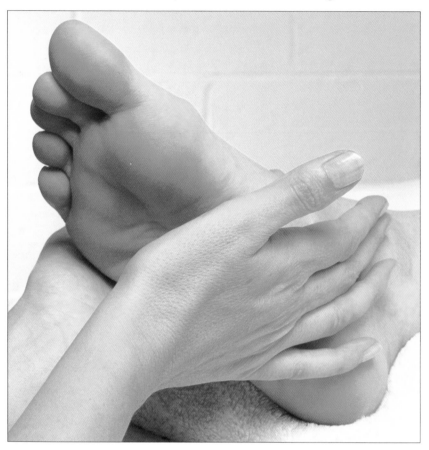

Gentle effleurage or stroking can help to relax the receiver if **they** have experienced a strong reaction during a treatment.

I must emphasize that strong reactions are very rare, but it is still a good idea to be prepared for everything. In the event of a continued emotional reaction, it is important never to panic and not to break off contact with the receiver. Offer paper tissues if appropriate and wait quietly until they have calmed themselves and settled down. If they feel that they want to talk about the emotions that have been released, allow them to do to. Try to listen with empathy and without interruption, offering reassurance when necessary. If they do not wish to verbalize their feelings, their wishes should be respected. You may want to offer them a glass of water and perhaps even a few drops of "Rescue Remedy."

Once the reaction has subsided, bring the treatment to a close with some gentle effleurage and the solar-plexus release described at the end of the step-by-step section of this book.

POSSIBLE REACTIONS BETWEEN TREATMENTS

- a state of deep relaxation
- an alteration in sleeping patterns, eventually leading to deep sleep
- more frequent and memorable dreams
- emotional changes and a greater awareness of feelings
- increased skin activity – pimples, rashes, and increased perspiration – the skin tone and texture eventually improve
- increase in urination
- cloudy or unpleasant-smelling urine
- the bowels move more frequently
- increase in bulk and volume of the stools
- nasal discharge
- coughing and secretions from the bronchi
- colds
- sneezing
- watery eyes
- sore throat
- fever
- vaginal discharge
- toothache
- a need to drink more water to flush away t he toxins
- a healing crisis
- previous illnesses that have been suppressed may flare up temporarily and then disappear
- tiredness: feeling tired after a treatment is a common reaction; later, however, the receiver should expect to feel energized

How Much Pressure to Use

The amount of pressure that you should use will vary enormously from one individual to another. Try to develop your sensitivity and adjust your pressure accordingly.

Once again, use your common sense. If the receiver feels as if they are being tickled, you are using too little pressure. If the receiver pulls or jerks their feet away from you, you need to reduce the pressure. If you are not sure if you are using the correct amount of pressure, ask the receiver for feedback.

Remember that reflexology should *never* be painful. Do not assume that the more pain you inflict, the better the treatment. Reflexology should be a highly pleasurable experience: the receiver should fall asleep rather than grimace with pain.

Interestingly, I have found that more physical, earthy individuals seem to prefer a firm pressure, whereas more spiritual souls favor a much lighter treatment.

In general, you should expect to use more pressure on a healthy young adult than on a frail older person.

If you discover any tender reflexes on the feet, then perform *gentle* pressure circles over the area without causing undue discomfort. You should *never* work continuously on a reflex point for a long period of time. It is much more effective and pleasant for the receiver if you return to any tender areas at frequent intervals. As treatment progresses, the troublesome areas should eventually diminish and hopefully disappear.

BEFORE YOU COMMENCE, MAKE SURE THAT YOU:

1. Create the right ambience.
2. Position the receiver correctly.
3. Prepare yourself.
4. Carry out a physical examination.
5. Refresh the feet.
6. Check for any contraindications.

(Points 1 to 6 are covered in detail in Chapter 2.)

What the Receiver Will Feel

A treatment is an extremely relaxing and pleasurable experience. Many people will fall into the alpha state of relaxation, which is the level of consciousness at which healing takes place. Everyone is very different, but most people feel extremely relaxed, yet also light and revitalized, with a wonderful sense of well-being, at the end of a treatment.

Step-by-step Sequence

You are now ready to begin your first reflexology treatment.

Remember to create a soothing atmosphere that will enhance both your and the receiver's sense of relaxation and enjoyment of the treatment.

Every individual will have their own preferences as to how firm the pressure applied to their feet should be. Always be guided by their reaction.

Never use too much pressure when treating the receiver's feet. A reflexology treatment should never be painful.

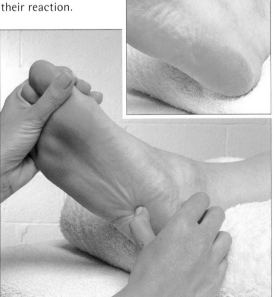

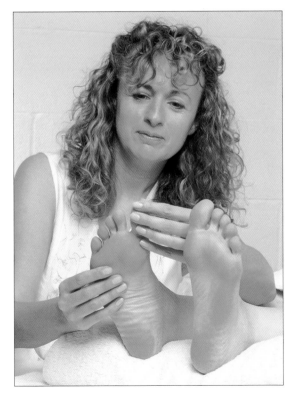

Once you have examined and refreshed the receiver's feet, you are ready to commence treatment.

Treating the Right Foot

The Warm-up

Because the foot that you are not working on should always be covered, ensure that the left foot is covered before beginning work on the right foot.

A full description of the relaxation techniques is given in Chapter 4.

Use any, or all, of the following techniques.

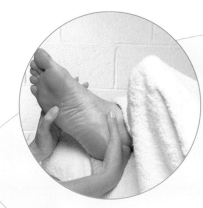

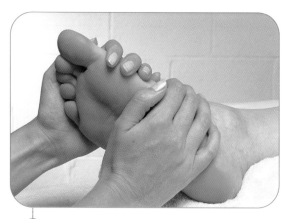

① **Greeting the Foot**

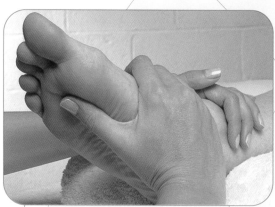

② **Stroking the Foot**

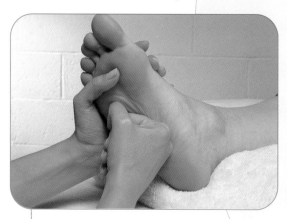

③ **Metatarsal-kneading**

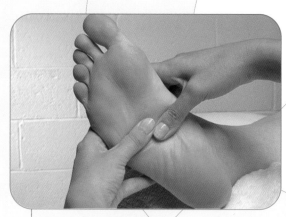

④ **Opening the Foot**

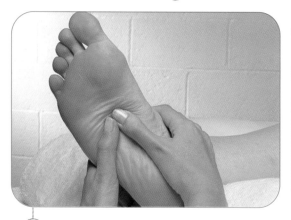

⑤ **Thumb-sliding**

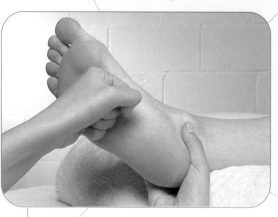

⑥ **Fist-sliding**

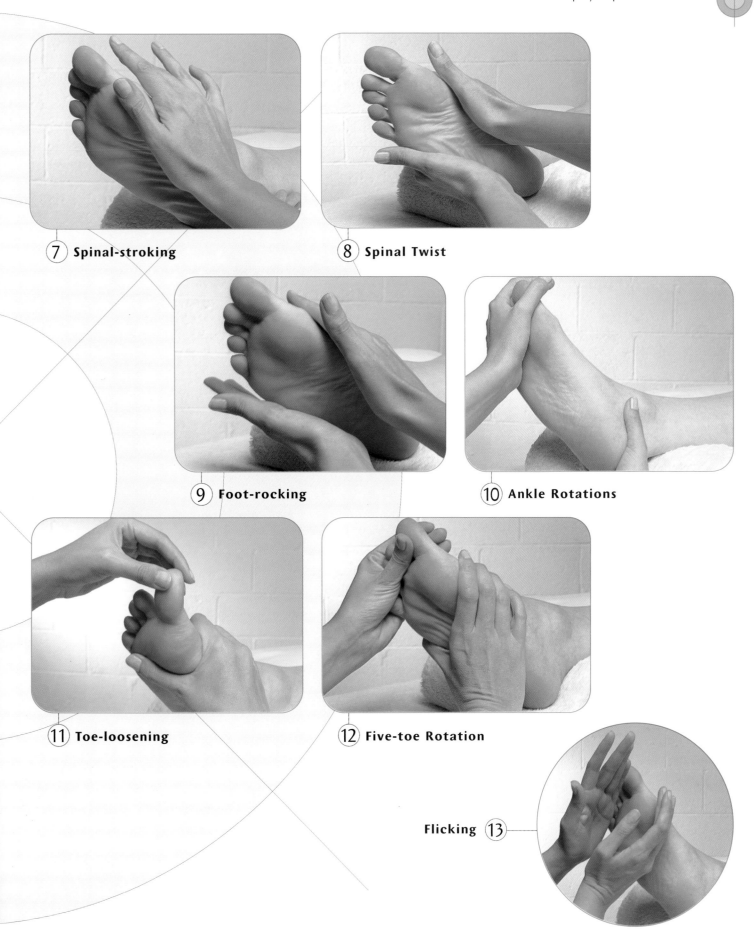

⑦ **Spinal-stroking**

⑧ **Spinal Twist**

⑨ **Foot-rocking**

⑩ **Ankle Rotations**

⑪ **Toe-loosening**

⑫ **Five-toe Rotation**

Flicking ⑬

The Head, Brain, and Neck Reflexes

These reflexes are located in the first transverse zone above the shoulder girdle line, which is found just below the base of the toes.

THE HEAD AND BRAIN

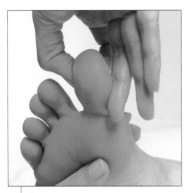

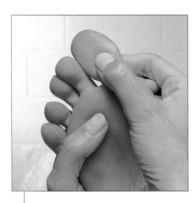

① This area is located on the top, back, and sides of the big toe. To treat the sides of the head and top of the brain, place the heel of your left hand around the outer aspect of the foot. Wrap the fingers of your left hand over the front of the toes and your thumb under the back of the toes. Using your right thumb, "walk" from the outer edge of the base of the big toe up the outside of the toe.

② Now thumb-walk over the top and down the inside of the big toe. Repeat this movement

③ To work on the back of the head, "walk" up the back of the big toe from the base to the tip. You will probably need to walk up the big toe four to six times to cover the entire area. If you prefer, you may walk down the big toe instead of up it. As you are working on such a small area, you will need to take tiny little "steps."

INDICATIONS

- headaches
- migraine
- memory defects
- Alzheimer's disease
- Parkinson's disease
- lack of concentration
- multiple sclerosis
- neuralgia
- learning problems, such as dyslexia
- attention-deficit disorder
- scalp problems

THE PITUITARY GLAND

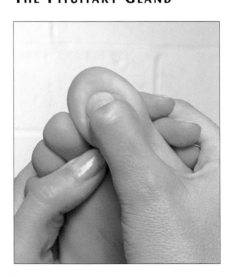

To find the pituitary-gland reflex point, locate the widest point on each side of the big toe and imagine a line stretching across these points. The pituitary-gland area is found approximately at the midpoint of this line. (You will often have to search to find this point. Sometimes a small lump is visible or palpable, indicating the location of the reflex.) Place the fingers of your left hand over the front of the toes and your thumb under the back of the toes. With the corner of your right thumb, use the hook-in and back-up technique on the pituitary-gland reflex. Ensure that your thumbnail is not digging into the big toe. This is often a very sensitive point, particularly if the receiver has a hormonal problem. If this reflex point is tender, use less pressure.

INDICATIONS

- hormonal problems

THE PINEAL GLAND/HYPOTHALAMUS

INDICATIONS

● pineal gland: S.A.D. (seasonal affective disorder)

● hypothalamus: hormonal problems

1 Move up your thumb slightly from the pituitary gland. Rock your thumb on to its outer edge and gently circle it over the area several times. This is the pineal-gland area.

2 Now rock your thumb on to its inner edge and gently circle it over the hypothalamus area.

THE OCCIPUT/MASTOID/TEMPLE

INDICATIONS

● headaches

● ear problems

Place your right thumb on the base of the big toe, close to the inner edge. Perform three tiny caterpillar-walks, moving upward, toward the tip of the toe.

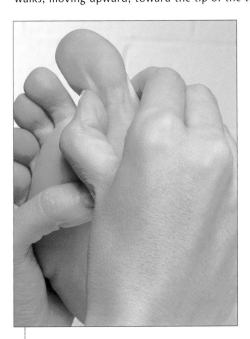

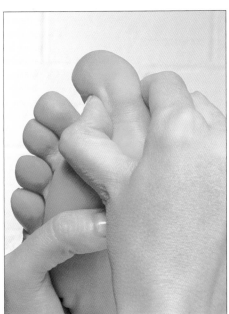

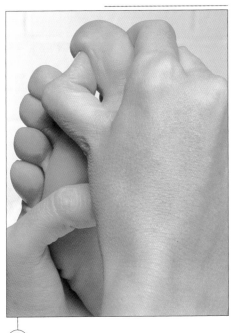

1 Stop and press into the occiput area.

2 Continue with just one step up the big toe to press into the mastoid area.

3 Use two more tiny steps to treat the temple area.

THE FACE

- eyes
- nose
- teeth
- gums
- lips
- jaw and facial problems, such as neuralgia
- acne

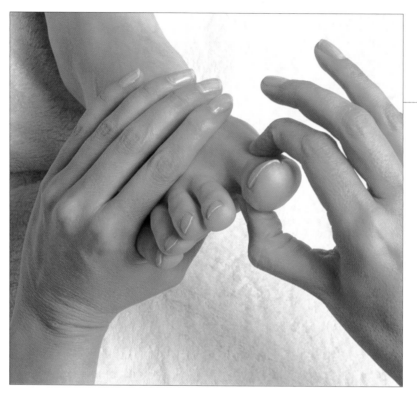

1. Wrap your left hand around the top of the foot, with your thumb underneath and your fingers on top. Using your right index finger, or index and middle fingers, "walk" down the front of the big toe, from the tip to the base. Caterpillar-walk downward as many times as is necessary to cover the whole of the front of the toe.

2. Alternatively, to treat the face, you may walk *across* the big toe, using two or more fingers.

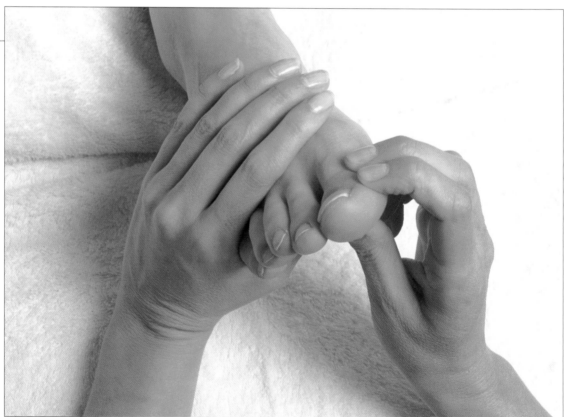

THE NECK

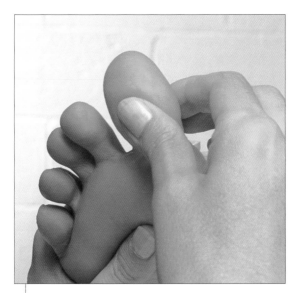

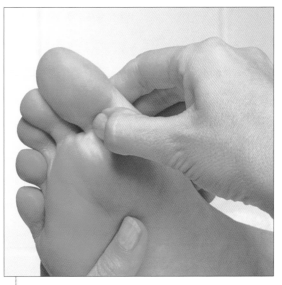

INDICATIONS

- neck problems
- throat disorders, such as tonsillitis
- laryngitis
- overuse of the vocal chords

1 Rotating the big toe will help to alleviate stiffness in the neck. Support the foot with your left hand, hold the big toe between the thumb and index finger of your right hand, and rotate the toe clockwise and anticlockwise. Perform this movement slowly and very gently. Do not force the big toe. If it grinds, cracks, or does not move very well, a problem with the neck is indicated.

2 To loosen the neck further, gently grasp the big toe between the thumb and fingers of your left hand. Using your right thumb, "walk" across the back of the base of the toe, from the outside to the inside, to treat the back of the neck.

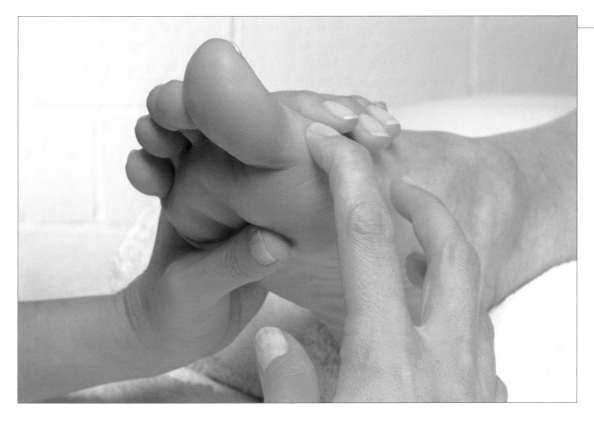

3 Using your index finger, "walk" across the front base of the big toe, working from the outside to the inside.

THE SINUSES

INDICATIONS

- sinusitis
- hayfever
- allergies
- catarrh

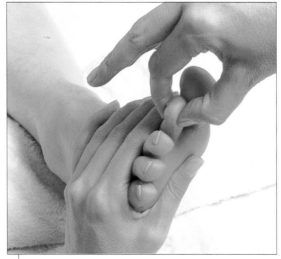

① The sinus areas are found down the center and both sides of the small toes. Support the right foot between the thumb and fingers of your left hand, with your thumb on the sole of the foot and your fingers over the front of the toes for support and control. Starting at the top of each toe, and using very small steps, thumb-walk down the back of each toe.

② When treating the sides of the toes, you may use either your thumb or index finger or else both together.

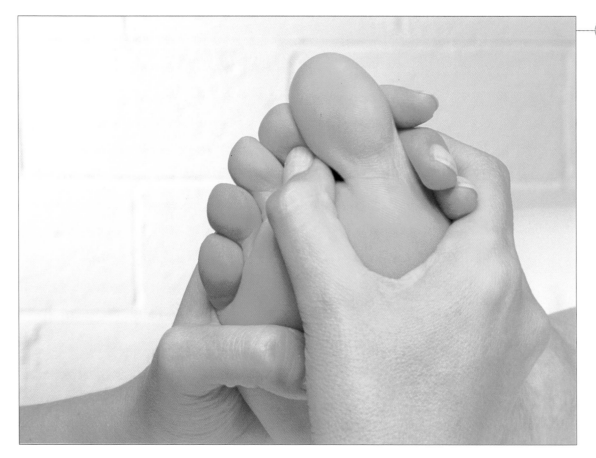

③ This technique can also be performed by working up the back and sides of the toes, instead of downward.

THE TEETH

Start at the base of the nail and finger-walk down the front of all five toes, covering the center and both sides of each toe. When walking down the big toe, you are giving a general treatment to all of the teeth. Toe two treats the incisors and canines, toe three the premolars, toe four the molars, and toe five the wisdom teeth.

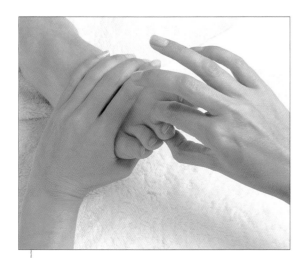

1 Here treatment is being given to toe three, treating the premolars.

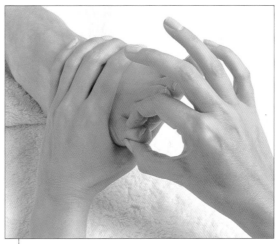

2 Finger-walking down the front of toe five treats the wisdom teeth.

THE UPPER LYMPHATICS

The reflex areas of the upper lymph nodes are found in the webbing between the toes. Support the foot with your left hand, and, using the thumb and index finger of your right hand, gently squeeze the webbing between each of the toes.

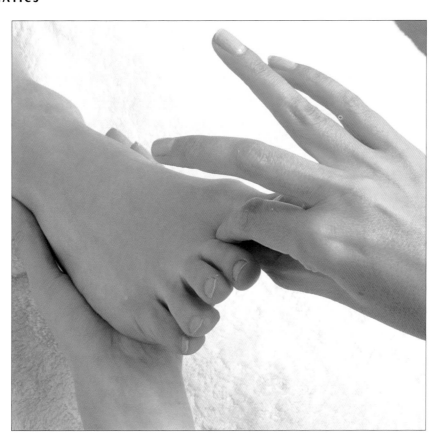

THE EYES, EARS, AND EUSTACHIAN TUBE

INDICATIONS

- watery eyes
- sore eyes
- tired eyes
- conjunctivitis
- glaucoma
- earache
- hearing problems
- balance problems
-

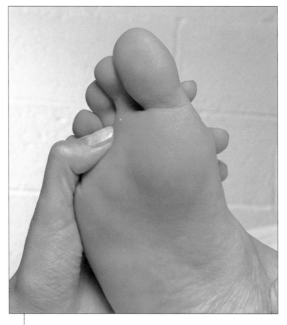

① The eyes, ears, and Eustachian-tube areas are found along the ridge at the base of the toes. To work this area, thumb-walk across the ridge, moving in both directions.

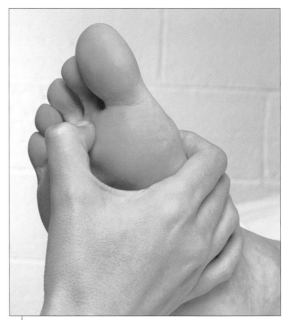

② To locate the right eye more precisely, caterpillar-walk across the ridge and stop between the second and third toes. Use your thumb either to hook in and back up or to perform pressure circles on the eye point.

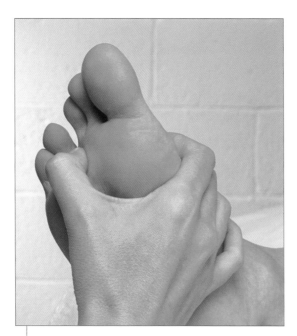

③ To treat the Eustachian tube, take a few more steps and stop between toes three and four. Now press firmly into this area.

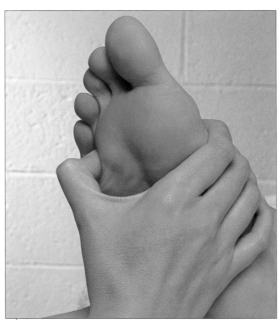

④ Continue to caterpillar-walk and stop between the fourth and fifth toes. Once again, either hook in and back up or use pressure circles to treat the right ear.

The Inner Edge of the Foot

THE SPINE

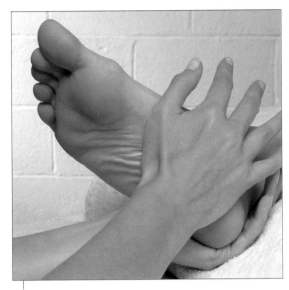

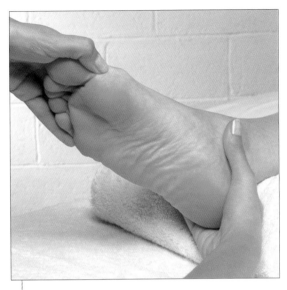

1 The reflexes of the spine are found along the inside edge of the foot, from the base of the nail bed down to the heel. To relax the spine, first support the right foot in the palm of your left hand and stroke down the inside of the foot with the heel of your hand, working from the big toe down to the heel.

2 Support the foot under the heel with your holding hand and caterpillar-walk down the inside of the foot, beginning at the base of the toenail. This represents the top of the spine (the cervical area).

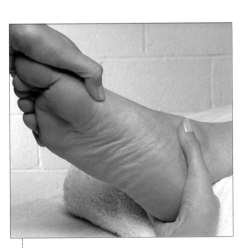

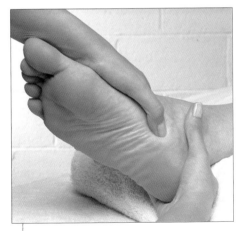

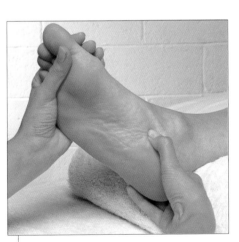

3 As you walk down the foot, you are covering the middle of the back (the thoracic area).

4 By working on the bottom of the foot you are covering the lower back (the lumbar area).

5 Now change hands, placing your holding hand at the top of the foot, with your thumb on the back of the toes and your fingers wrapped around the front. Repeat the thumb-walking procedure, working in the opposite direction, from the base of the heel up to the base of the toenail.

The Shoulder Girdle to Diaphragm Line

THE THYROID/PARATHYROIDS/THYMUS

The thyroid, parathyroids, and thymus reflex points are located on the ball of the foot, beneath the big toe. To perform a general treatment on these reflexes, support the right foot with your left hand.

INDICATIONS

- thyroid: thyroid problems
- weight problems
- nervousness
- palpitations
- dry skin
- lethargy
- the menopause
- parathyroids: osteoporosis
- arthritis
- muscle spasms
- thymus: immune system

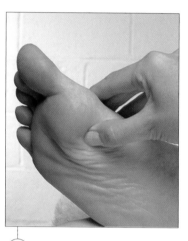

(1) Place your right thumb just below the ball of the foot on the inside, and thumb-walk upward from the diaphragm line.

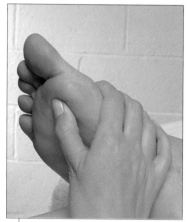

(2) Thumb-walk in a curved direction until your thumb is between the big toe and the second toe.

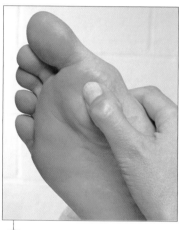

(3) Return to the diaphragm line and caterpillar-walk up the foot several times, until you have completely covered the area under the big toe.

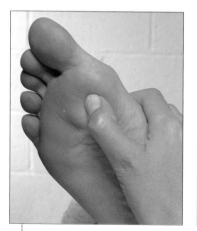

(4) The thyroid area is located in the center of the pad of the ball of the foot below the big toe. This reflex is often tender. Place the flat pad of your thumb on the thyroid area and gently circle your thumb over it several times. Any tenderness should diminish after a few pressure circles.

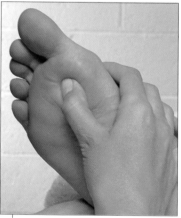

(5) The parathyroids area is found slightly to the left of that of the thyroid gland. Move your thumb slightly to the left and upward and then perform circles on the parathyroids area.

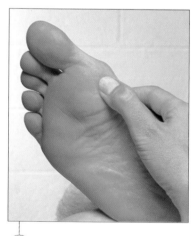

(6) The thymus area is found to the right of that of the thyroid gland, close to the spinal reflexes. Move your thumb to the right and very slightly downward, and then circle it over the thymus area.

THE RIGHT LUNG

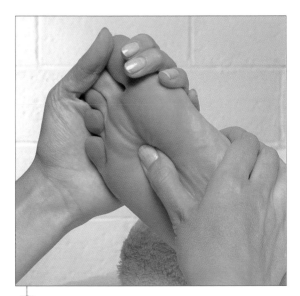

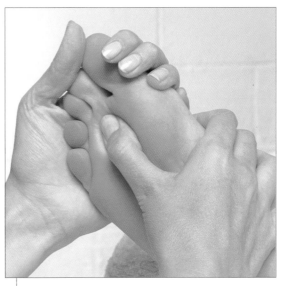

INDICATIONS

- all lung problems, such as coughs and colds
- chest infections
- asthma
- bronchitis
- emphysema
- shallow breathing
- hyperventilation and panic attacks

1 The lung area encompasses the ball of the foot, from the shoulder girdle line to the diaphragm line. Pull back the toes using your left holding hand, with your fingers cupped over the front of the toes and your thumb at the back. Start at the base of the toes and, using your right thumb, caterpillar-walk in vertical strips from the diaphragm line to the shoulder girdle line on the sole of the foot.

2 Thumb-walk until the whole of the area between the shoulder girdle line and the diaphragm line has been covered.

3 You may also work this area by caterpillar-walking across the foot in horizontal, instead of vertical, strips.

THE RIGHT BREAST/LUNGS/RIBS/MAMMARY GLANDS

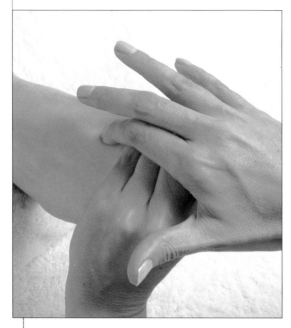

(1) Pull the toes forward with your left hand, with your thumb under the sole of the foot and your fingers cupped over the top of the toes. Finger-walk down the troughs on the top of the foot, from the base of the toes to the diaphragm line. Cover the entire area in vertical strips. As the top of the foot is more sensitive, use your index finger to do the walking.

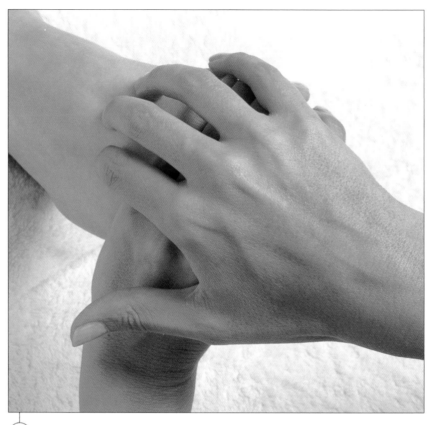

(2) You may also use several fingers at once. This will enable you to cover the whole of this sensitive area quickly and effectively.

INDICATIONS

- lung problems
- breast problems, such as tenderness due to P.M.T.
- harmless lumps that have been investigated

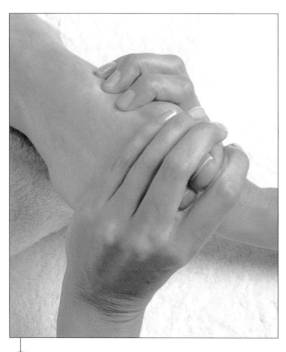

(3) If you wish, you may also "walk" across this area in horizontal strips.

(4) You can also support the foot by making a fist with your left hand and placing it under the toes; now finger-walk as described previously.

THE SHOULDER

When you treated the right lung, you were also inadvertently treating the right shoulder. The reflex for the shoulder is partly located between the shoulder girdle and the diaphragm line in zone five under the little toe. It is also found on the lateral (outer) edge at the base of the little toe.

INDICATIONS

- aches and pains in the shoulder
- arthritis
- inflammatory
- conditions, such as bursitis and tendonitis

Place your thumb ① on the outside edge of the little toe and perform pressure circles to treat the area under the toe's lateral edge.

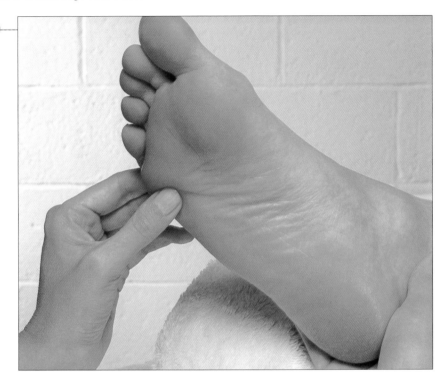

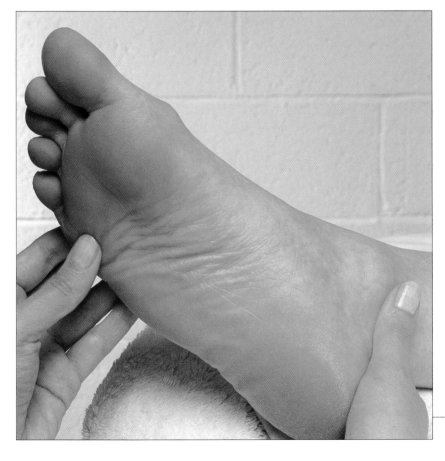

② Now perform pressure circles at the lateral edge of the little toe.

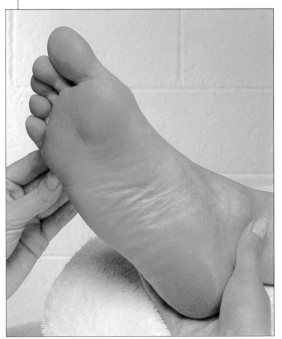

③ This area usually needs attention, as it will often feel "gritty" and congested.

The Diaphragm Line to the Waist Line

THE LIVER/GALLBLADDER (RIGHT FOOT ONLY)

INDICATIONS

- digestive disturbances
- toxic individuals
- liver problems, such as jaundice and gallbladder problems

Imagine a triangle extending upward, across the diaphragm line from the left-hand side of the diaphragm line to the left-hand side of the waist line and then across to the right-hand side of the diaphragm line. Bend the toes away from you to open up the reflex area and caterpillar-walk the liver area in diagonal strips.

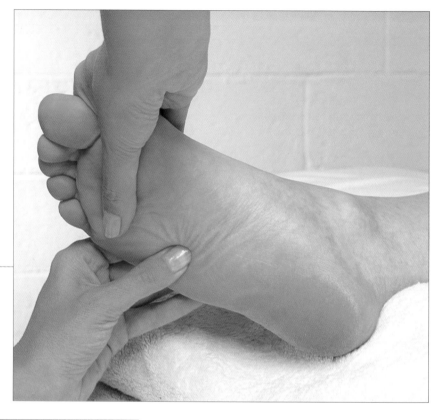

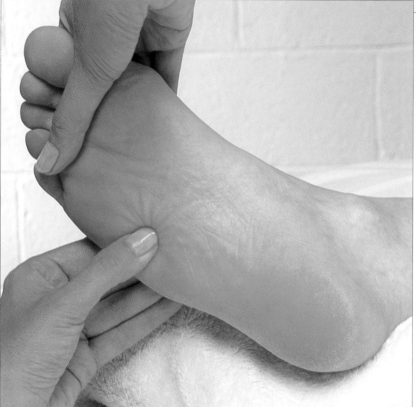

② Locate the gallbladder reflex, which lies between the diaphragm line and the waist line, in line with the fourth toe. The gallbladder reflex appears to vary somewhat in its location, but can feel like an indentation or small swelling. As this is often a tender point, use the rotation technique. Support the foot with your right hand and place the pad of your left thumb on the gallbladder reflex. With your right, holding hand, slowly flex the foot into your left thumb and rotate the foot in a circular motion around the thumb. Interestingly, if the gallbladder has been removed, a "hole" can often be felt.

THE STOMACH/PANCREAS/DUODENUM

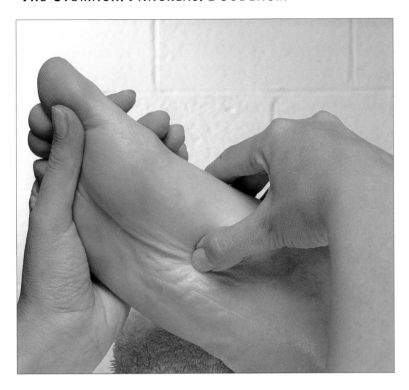

The stomach, pancreas, and duodenum may be treated by working on the sole of the right foot, as well as the left foot. Use your left hand to hold the foot and thumb-walk just below the diaphragm line, from the inside of the foot (zone one) to approximately the center of the foot (zone two). Repeat the caterpillar-walking in horizontal rows until you reach the waist line. You may reverse your hands to work in the opposite direction if you wish.

INDICATIONS

- stomach: indigestion
- heartburn
- ulcers and stomach cramps
- pancreas: digestive disorders
- diabetes
- hypoglycemia (low blood sugar)

THE ADRENAL GLAND

The adrenal gland is usually easily pinpointed, as it is often tender. If you pull back the toes, a thick tendon will protrude, running from the big toe to the heel. The adrenal reflex point is located approximately midway between the diaphragm and the waist line, on the medial side (inside) of this tendon.

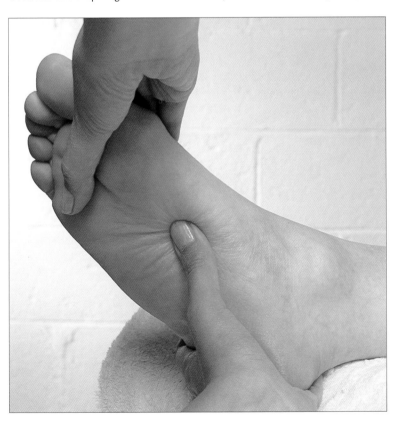

INDICATIONS

- all nervous disorders
- inflammatory conditions, particularly rheumatoid arthritis
- allergies, especially asthma
- lack of energy and exhaustion
- pain relief

With your right hand holding the right foot, and your fingers wrapped around the top, place your left thumb on the adrenal point. Use your right hand to flex the foot on to your left thumb and then rotate the foot around it..

Below the Waist Line

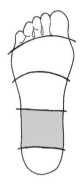

THE RIGHT KIDNEY/URETER TUBE/BLADDER

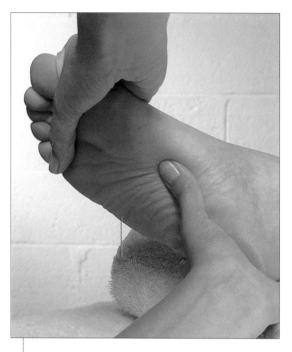

(1) Part of the kidney reflex is located just above the waist line, between zones two and three. The other half of the kidney, ureter-tube, and bladder areas is located below the waist line. After you have gently rotated the adrenal reflex, move your thumb down slightly and you will have found the kidney reflex point on the waist line. With the tip of your thumb pointing toward the toes, press into the area and circle your thumb gently over it several times.

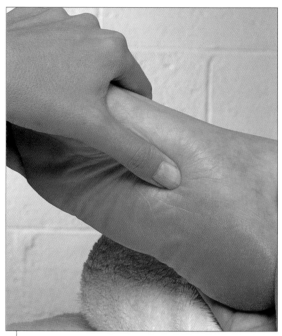

(2) Turn your thumb around so that it is facing downward and then caterpillar-walk down the ureter reflex toward the inside of the foot, where the bladder reflex is situated beneath the inner ankle bone.

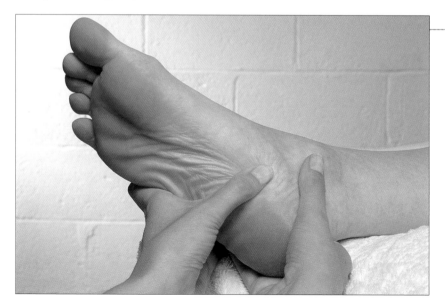

(3) The bladder area can often look slightly puffy, particularly if a woman is premenstrual. Either thumb-walk over, or perform pressure circles on, the bladder reflex.

THE SMALL INTESTINE

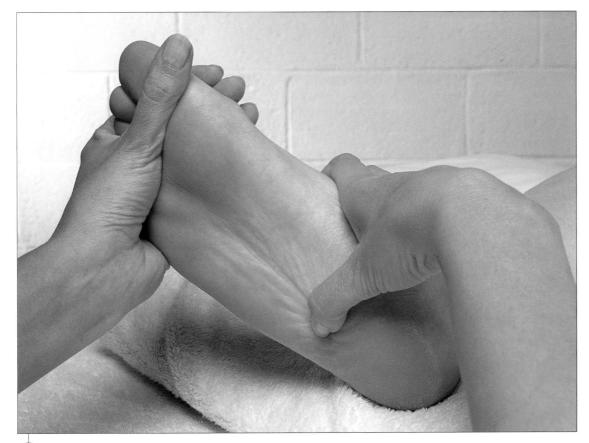

● digestive problems

● abdominal cramps

 1 Hold back the right foot with your left hand and caterpillar-walk in horizontal rows from just below the waist line to the pelvic-floor line, from the medial aspect (inside) of the foot as far as zone four.

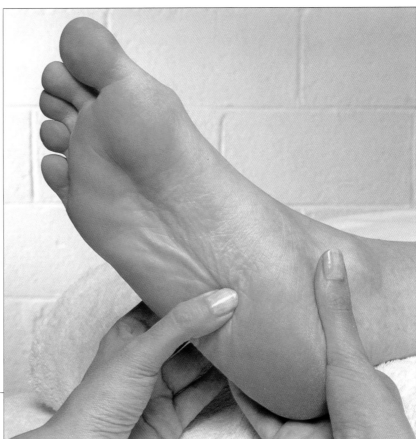

You may work on the whole of this area in the opposite direction The more comfortable and confident your hands feel, the more effective your treatment will be. 2

THE APPENDIX/ILEOCECAL VALVE/ASCENDING AND TRANSVERSE COLON

INDICATIONS

- digestive problems, such as constipation
- diarrhea
- irritable-bowel syndrome
- Crohn's disease
- celiac disease

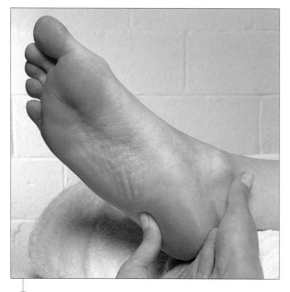

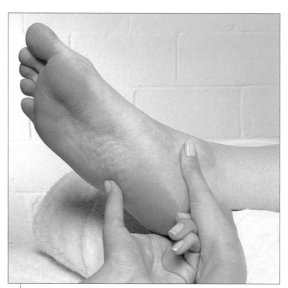

(1) The colon wraps around the small intestine. To locate the appendix/ileocecal valve, run your finger along zones four and five, down the lower third of the sole of the foot toward the heel. Just above the pelvic-floor line, you may feel a hollow spot. Using your left thumb, press on the point and circle over the reflex area several times .

(2) Using your left thumb, caterpillar-walk up the ascending-colon area in zones four and five toward the waist line. You may feel a swelling either on, or just below, the waist line, which is the hepatic flexure, where the colon bends to continue as the transverse colon. Circle over this area several times.

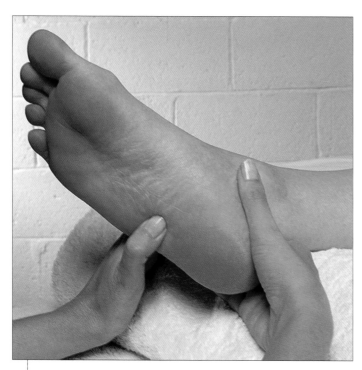

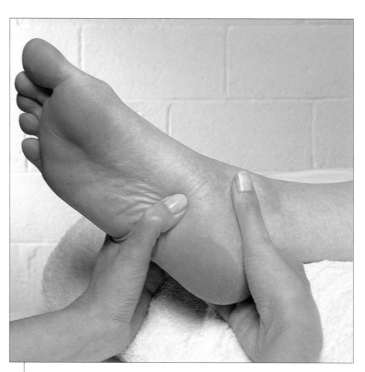

(3) Now turn your thumb 90° to the right and caterpillar-walk horizontally along the transverse-colon reflex.

(4) Follow the waist line until you reach the inside of the sole of the foot. If the receiver has constipation, repeat this movement several times.

The Outer Aspect of the Foot

THE JOINTS: RIGHT SHOULDER/ARM/ELBOW/HAND/HIP/KNEE AND LEG

The areas corresponding to the joints of the body are situated along the outer edge of the foot. (Remember that the spine area runs the length of the inside of the foot.)

INDICATIONS

- all joint problems, including arthritis
- sports injuries, such as tennis elbow
- stiff shoulder
- housemaid's knee
- cartilage and ligament problems

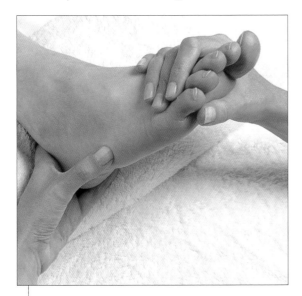

1 Hold the toes of the right foot with your right hand. Using your left thumb, caterpillar-walk vertically up the outer edge of the foot, from the heel area to the little toe. If you wish, you may cup the right heel with your left hand and repeat the thumb-walking in the opposite direction, from the little toe to the heel.

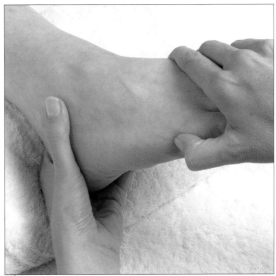

2 If you come across any areas that are tender, gently circle your thumb over them several times. The shoulder reflex on the bony prominence at the base of the little toe is likely to need attention. Perform some pressure circles over this reflex.

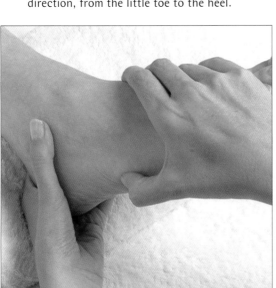

3 The protrusion farther down on the side of the foot is the knee reflex. Perform several pressure circles.

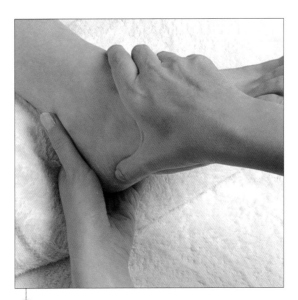

4 Slightly farther down is the hip reflex.

Around the Ankles

THE SCIATIC-NERVE LINE/PELVIC AREA

The area around the Achilles tendon is not only worked for problems with the sciatic nerve, but also for chronic ailments related to the prostate, uterus, and rectum.

INDICATIONS

- sciatica
- lower-back and hip problems
- chronic problems with the uterus
- prostate and rectum problems

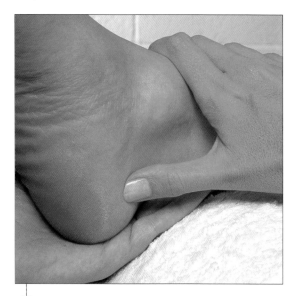

1 Hold the right foot with your left hand and place your right thumb above the inner ankle bone. Now thumb-walk down the Achilles-tendon area toward the heel.

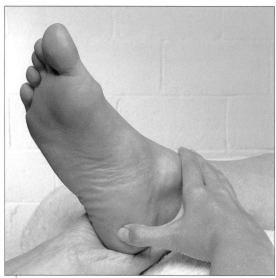

2 Continue to thumb-walk across the sciatic-nerve line, which is found on the hard heel pad of the right foot.

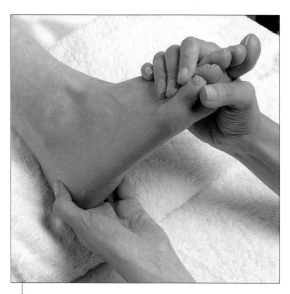

3 Finger- or thumb-walk up the outside of the foot along the Achilles-tendon line, changing hands if necessary.

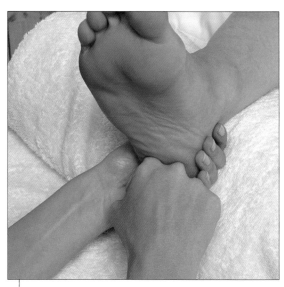

4 If the receiver has pelvic problems, working across the heel pad can be very effective. Cup the foot with your left hand and gently work the area with your knuckles, moving in a circular direction.

THE RIGHT TESTICLE/OVARY

- infertility problems
- menstrual irregularities
- ovarian cysts
- the menopause

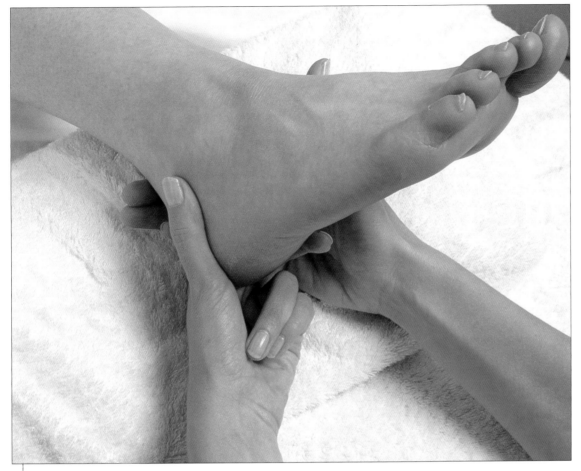

1 All of the reproductive-organ reflexes are situated around the ankle area. If the receiver is pregnant, the reproductive areas should be avoided if you are not a professional reflexologist. (A fully qualified reflexologist will use stroking movements over the uterus and ovary reflexes.) Locate the testicle/ovary reflex by drawing an imaginary diagonal line from the outer anklebone to the top of the heel and then finding the midpoint. The ovary reflex is illustrated here.

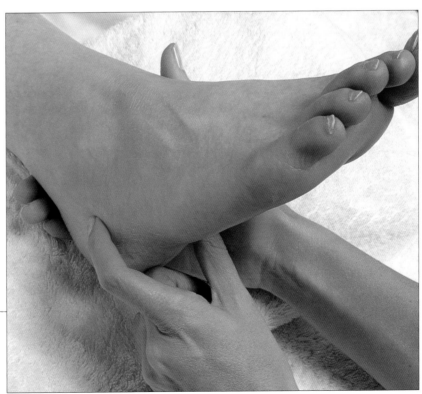

Now perform small, circular movements over **2** this area using your index finger. (Remember to avoid this area if the receiver is pregnant and you are not a professional reflexologist.)

THE FALLOPIAN TUBES/VAS DEFERENS/LYMPH AND GROIN

Thumb- or finger-walk from the outside of the ankle across the top of the foot to the inside of the ankle.

- problems with the male or female reproductive organs
- swelling of the feet

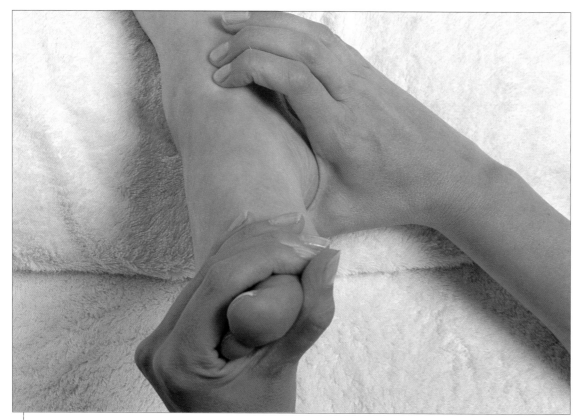

(1) This area may be "walked'"in both directions. Here finger-walking is demonstrated over the Fallopian-tube/lymph/groin reflex.

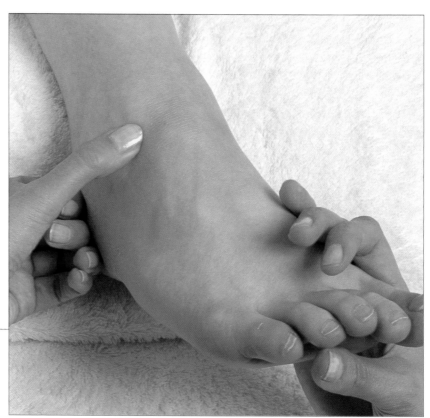

This can be quite a sensitive area, so if you find (2) a tender spot, gently massage it in a circular direction. If the area is tender, it is likely to be indicate a clogged-up lymphatic system.

THE PROSTATE/UTERUS

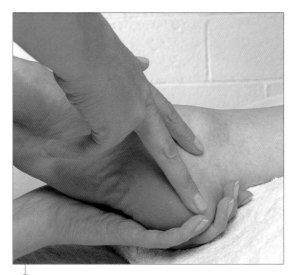

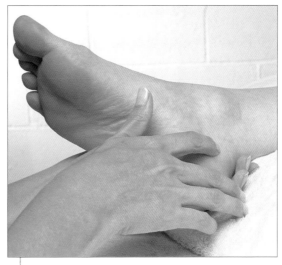

- all menstrual problems
- painful, irregular periods
- scanty or heavy periods
- fertility problems
- P.M.T.
- the menopause
- prostate problems

① To locate the prostate/uterus point, place your index finger on the inner anklebone and your second finger on the tip of the heel. Imagine a straight line running between your fingers. The prostate/uterus lies in the middle of this imaginary line. The uterus reflex is being worked on here.

② Place your index finger on the point and perform small pressure circles. (The index finger is used because this is often a tender area.)

THE FINALE

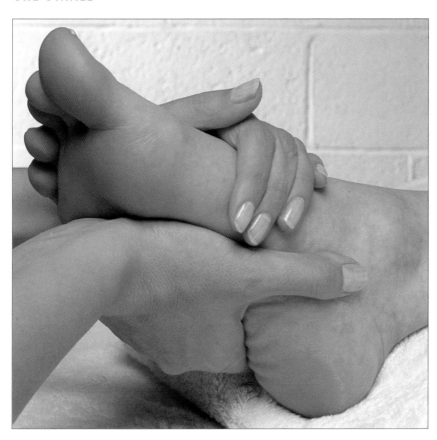

Using both hands, stroke the whole of the right foot, working from the toes, gliding around the anklebones, and then moving back again. Repeat these movements several times to ensure that any toxins that have been released during the reflexology sequence are dispersed and that the foot is totally relaxed. Now cover up the right foot.

Treating the Left Foot

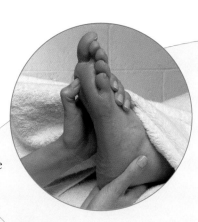

The Warm-up

Remember that the foot that you are not working on should always be covered, so now cover the right foot and uncover the left.

Refer to Chapter 4 for a full description of the relaxation techniques. Any, or all, of the following techniques can be used.

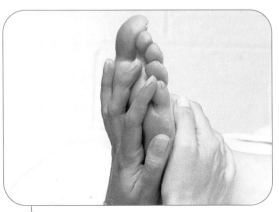

① **Greeting the Foot**

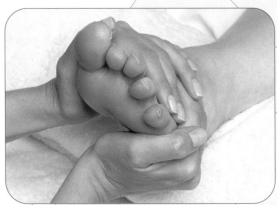

② **Stroking the Foot**

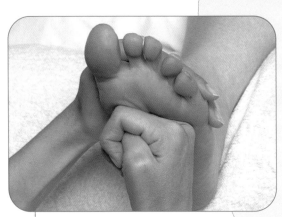

③ **Metatarsal-kneading**

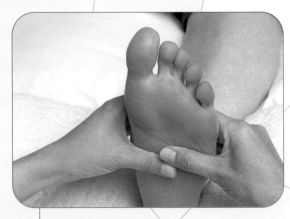

④ **Opening the Foot**

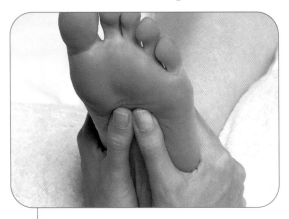

⑤ **Thumb-sliding**

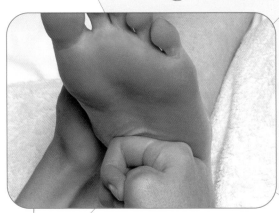

⑥ **Fist-sliding**

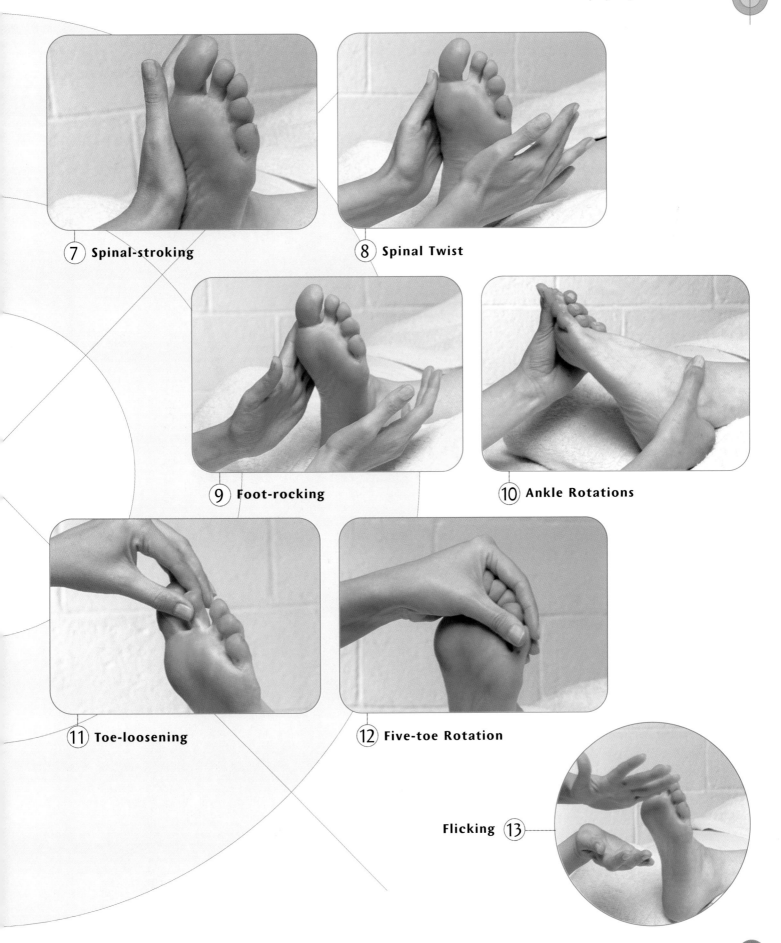

⑦ **Spinal-stroking**

⑧ **Spinal Twist**

⑨ **Foot-rocking**

⑩ **Ankle Rotations**

⑪ **Toe-loosening**

⑫ **Five-toe Rotation**

Flicking ⑬

The Head, Brain, and Neck Reflexes

These reflexes are located in the first transverse zone above the shoulder girdle line, which is found just below the base of the toes.

THE HEAD AND BRAIN

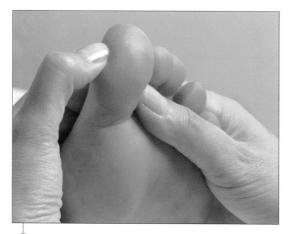

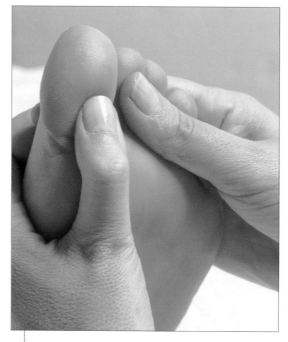

① This area is located on the top, back, and sides of the big toe. To treat the sides of the head and top of the brain, place the heel of your right hand around the outer aspect of the foot. Wrap the fingers of your right hand over the front of the toes and your thumb under the back. Using your left thumb, "walk" from the outer edge of the base of the big toe up the outside, over the top, and down the inside of the big toe. Repeat this movement

② To work on the back of the head, "walk" up the back of the big toe, from the base to the tip. You will need to walk up the big toe several times to cover the entire area.

INDICATIONS

- headaches
- migraine
- memory defects
- Alzheimer's disease
- Parkinson's disease
- lack of concentration
- multiple sclerosis
- neuralgia
- learning problems, such as dyslexia
- attention-deficit disorder
- scalp problems

If you prefer, you may walk down the big toe ③ instead of up it. As you are working on such a small area, you will need to take tiny "steps."

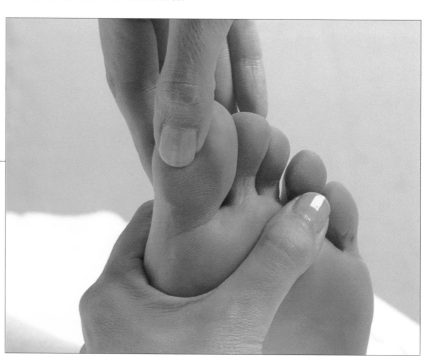

THE PITUITARY GLAND

● hormonal problems

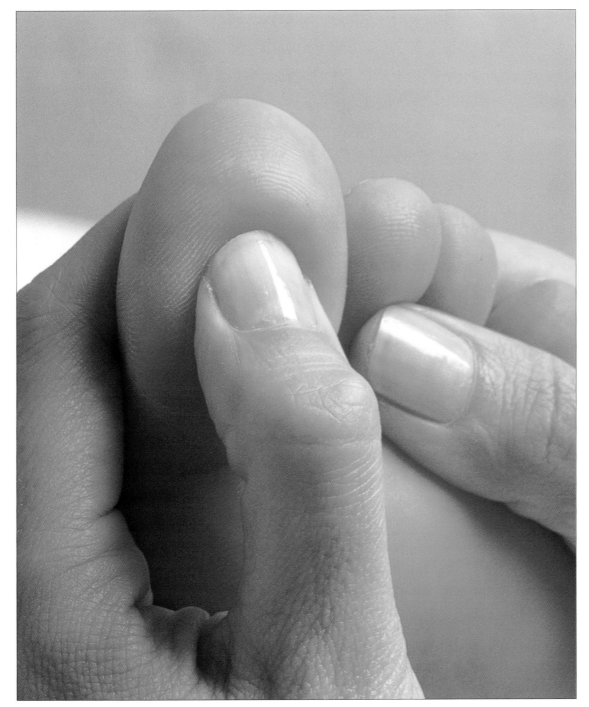

To find the pituitary-gland reflex point, locate the widest point on each side of the big toe and imagine a line stretching across these points. The pituitary-gland area is found approximately at the midpoint of this line. (You will often have to search to find this point. A small lump is sometimes visible or palpable, indicating the location of the pituitary-gland reflex.) Place the fingers of your right hand over the front of the toes and your thumb under the back. With the corner of your left thumb, use the hook-in and back-up technique on the pituitary-gland reflex. Ensure that your thumbnail is not digging into the big toe. This is often a very sensitive point, particularly if the receiver has a hormonal problem. If this reflex point is tender, use lless pressure.

THE PINEAL GLAND/HYPOTHALAMUS

INDICATIONS

- pineal gland:
  S.A.D. (seasonal
  affective disorder)
- hypothalamus:
  hormone problems

Move your left ①
thumb slightly up
from the pituitary-
gland area. Rock
your thumb on to
its outer edge and
gently circle over
the area several
times. This is the
pineal-gland reflex.

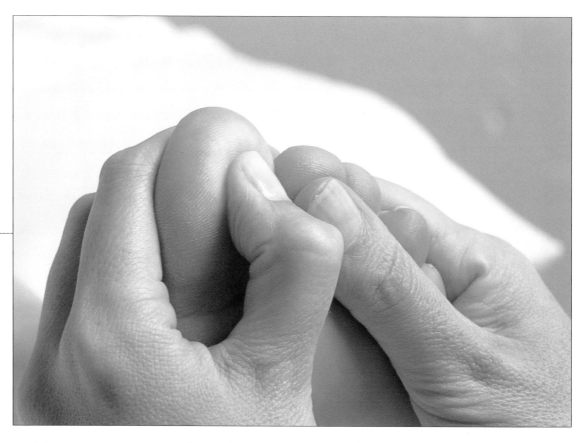

② Now rock your
thumb on to its
inner edge and
gently circle it
over the
hypothalamus
reflex point.

THE OCCIPUT/MASTOID/TEMPLE

Place your thumb at the base of the big toe, close to the inner edge. Perform three tiny caterpillar walks, moving upward, toward the tip of the toe.

- headaches
- ear problems

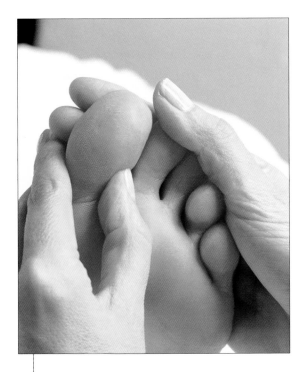

① Stop and press into the occiput area.

③ Use two more tiny steps to treat the temple area.

② Continue with just one step up the big toe to press into the mastoid area.

THE FACE

INDICATIONS

- eyes
- nose
- teeth
- gums
- lips
- jaw
- facial problems, such as neuralgia
- acne

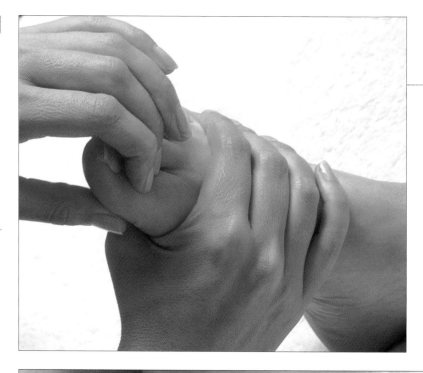

① Wrap your right hand around the top of the foot, with your thumb underneath and fingers on top. Using your left index finger, or index and middle fingers, "walk' down the front of the big toe, from the tip of the toe to the base. Caterpillar-walk downward as many times as is necessary to cover the whole of the front of the toe.

Alternatively, ② to treat the face, you may walk *across* the big toe, using your first two or three fingers.

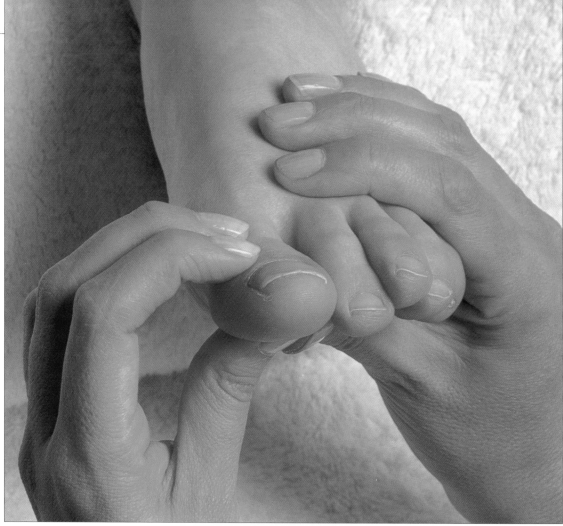

THE NECK

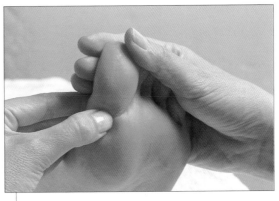

1. Rotating the big toe will help to alleviate stiffness in the neck. Support the foot with your right hand, hold the big toe between the thumb and index finger of your left hand, and rotate the toe clockwise and anticlockwise. Perform this movement slowly and very gently. Do not force the big toe. If the toe grinds, cracks, or does not move very well, it may indicate a problem with the neck.

2. To loosen the neck further, gently grasp the big toe between the thumb and fingers of your right hand. Using your left thumb, "walk" across the back of the base of the toe, from the outside the inside, to treat the back of the neck.

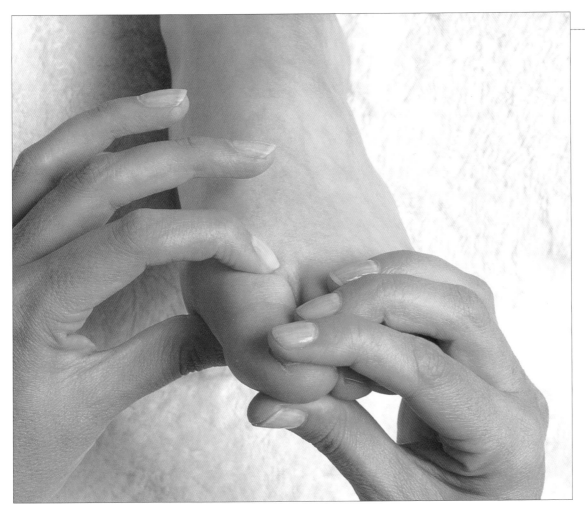

3. Using your index finger, "walk" across the front base of the big toe, working from the outside to the inside.

THE SINUSES

INDICATIONS

- sinusitis
- hayfever
- allergies
- catarrh

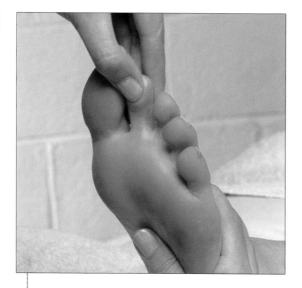

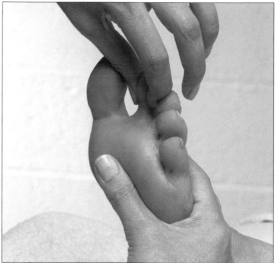

1. The sinuse areas are found down the center and both sides of the small toes. Support the left foot between the thumb and fingers of your right hand, with your thumb on the sole of the foot and your fingers over the front of the toes for support and control. Starting at the top of each toe, and using very small "steps," thumb-walk down the back of each toe.

2. When treating the sides of the toes, you may use either your thumb or index finger or else both together.

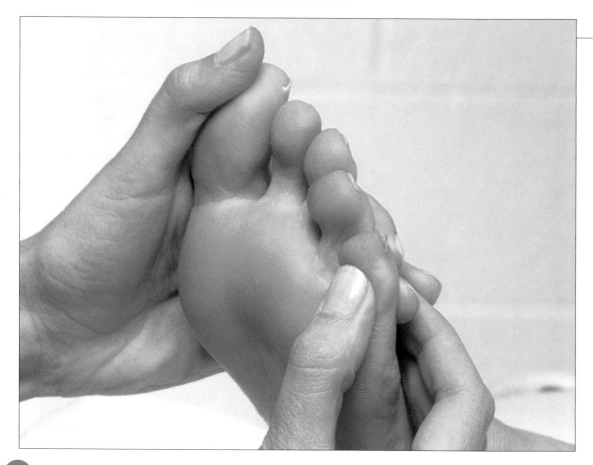

3. This technique can also be performed by working up the back and sides of the toes, instead of downward. However, it makes sense to "walk" down the toes so that you are draining toward the upper lymphatics.

THE TEETH

Start at the base of the nail and finger-walk down the fronts of all five toes, covering the center and both sides of each toe.

- toothache
- sensitive, painful, infected, or inflamed teeth and gums
- abscesses

When "walking" down the big toe, you are giving a general treatment to all of the teeth. Toe two treats the incisors and canines, toe three the premolars, toe four the molars, and toe five the wisdom teeth.

THE UPPER LYMPHATICS

The reflex areas of the upper lymph nodes are found in the webbing between the toes. Support the foot with your left hand, and, using the thumb and index finger of your right hand, gently squeeze the webbing between each of the toes.

INDICATIONS

- to prevent and fight off infections.

73

The Eyes, Ears, and Eustachian Tube

- Watery, sore, and tired eyes
- conjunctivitis
- glaucoma
- ears: earache
- infections
- hearing problems
- balance problems
-

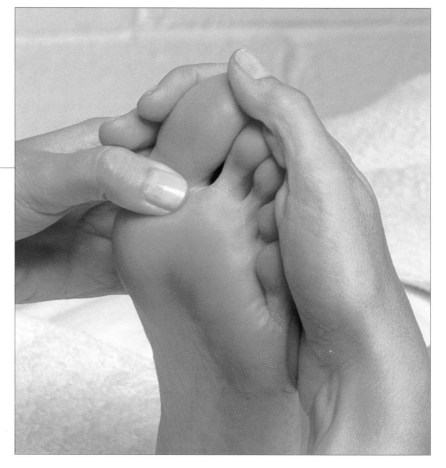

The eyes, ears, and **1** Eustachian-tube areas are found along the ridge at the base of the toes. Gently pull back the toes with your holding hand to make the area easy to reach, with your thumb at the bottom and your fingers at the top. Thumb-walk across the ridge. You may work in both directions.

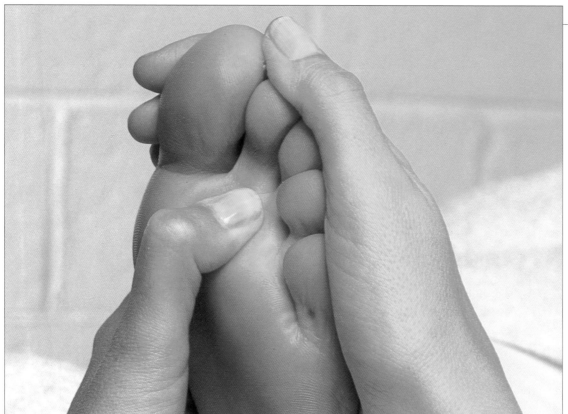

2 To locate the left eye more precisely, caterpillar-walk across the ridge and stop between the second and third toes. Use your thumb to hook in and back up or to perform pressure circles on the eye point.

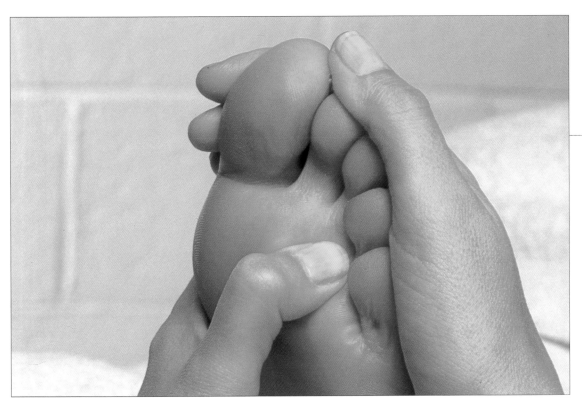

3 To treat the Eustachian-tube area, take a few more steps and stop between toes three and four. Press firmly into this area.

4 Continue to caterpillar-walk and stop between the fourth and fifth toes. Once again, either hook in and back up or use pressure circles to treat the left ear.

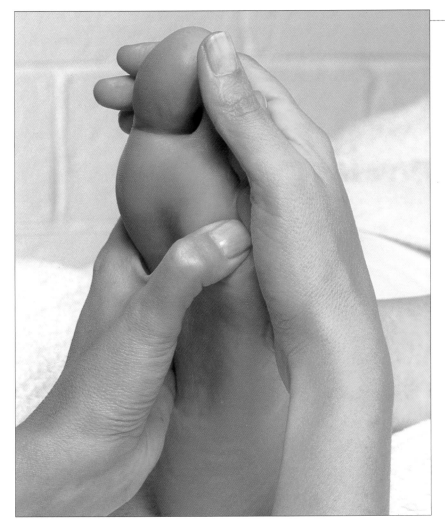

The Inner Edge of the Foot

THE SPINE

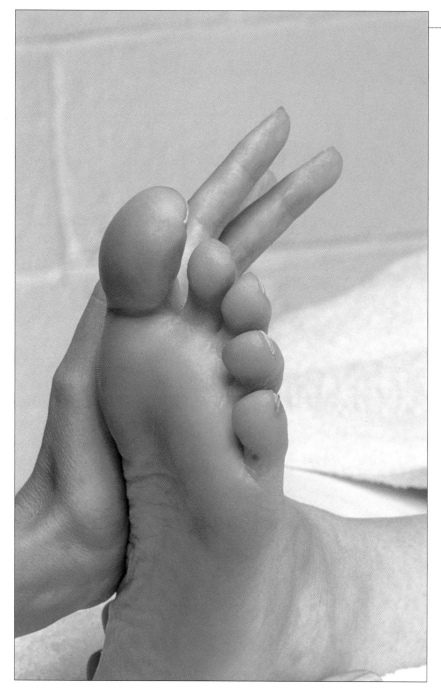

1 The reflexes of the spine are found along the inside edge of the foot, from the base of the nail bed down to the heel. To relax the spine, first support the left foot in the palm of your hand and stroke down the inside of the foot with the heel of your hand, working from the big toe down to the heel.

INDICATIONS

- back problems
- aches and pains
- stiffness
- arthritis

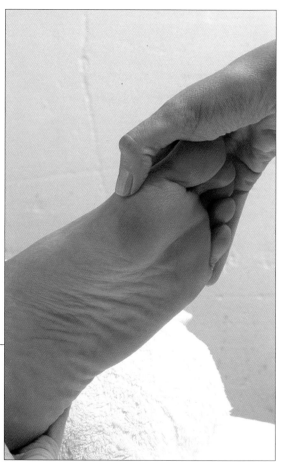

Support the foot under the heel with your holding hand and caterpillar-walk down the inside of the foot, beginning at the base of the toenail. This represents the top of the spine (the cervical area). **2**

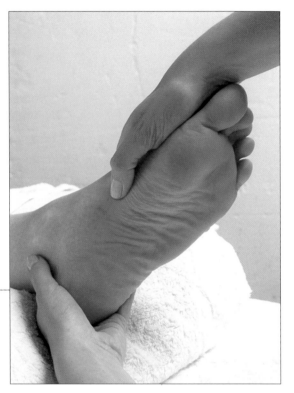

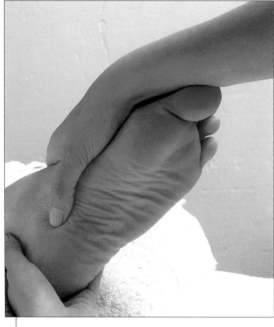

As you "walk" ③ down the foot, you are covering the middle of the back (the thoracic area).

④ Farther down, you will be covering the lower back (the lumbar area).

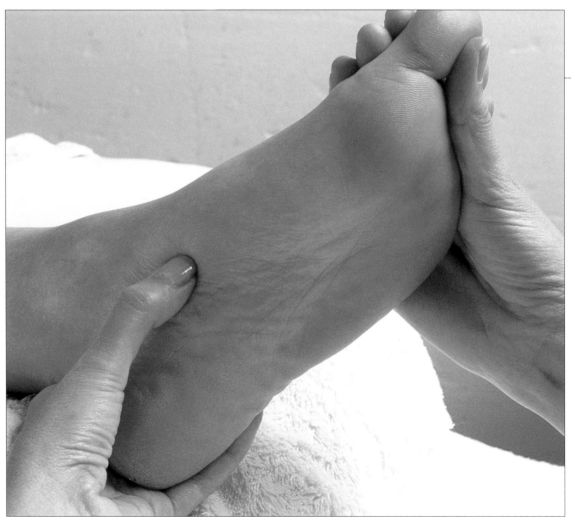

⑤ Now change hands, placing your holding hand at the top of the foot, with your thumb on the back of the toes and your fingers wrapped around the front. Repeat the thumb-walking procedure, working in the opposite direction, from the base of the heel up to the base of the toenail.

The Shoulder Girdle to Diaphragm Line

THE THYROID/PARATHYROIDS/THYMUS

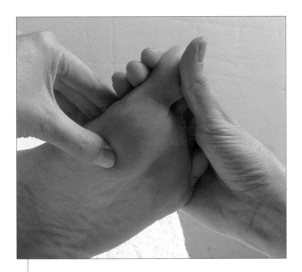

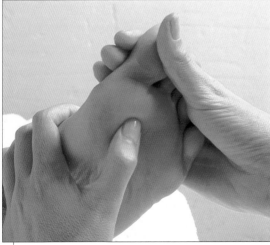

INDICATIONS

- thyroid: thyroid problems
- weight problems
- nervousness
- palpitations
- dry skin
- lethargy
- the menopause
- parathyroids: osteoporosis
- arthritis
- muscle spasms
- thymus: immune system

(1) The thyroid, parathyroids, and thymus reflex points are located on the ball of the foot, beneath the big toe. To perform a general treatment on these reflexes, support and hold back the toes of the left foot with your right hand. Place your left thumb just below the ball of the foot on the inside.

(2) Thumb-walk from the diaphragm line in a curved direction until your thumb is between the big toe and the second toe. Return to the diaphragm line and caterpillar-walk up the foot several times, until you have completely covered the area under the big toe.

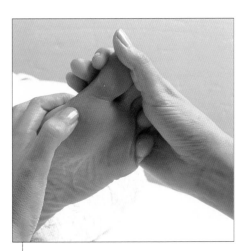

(3) The thyroid reflex is located in the center of the pad of the ball of the foot below the big toe. This reflex is often tender. Place the flat pad of your thumb on the thyroid area and gently circle your thumb over it several times. If there is any tenderness, this should diminish after a few pressure circles.

(4) The parathyroids area is found slightly to the right of that of the thyroid gland. Move your thumb slightly to the right and perform circles on the parathyroids area.

(5) The thymus area is found to the left of that of the thyroid gland, close to the spinal reflexes. Move your thumb to the left and again use it to circle over the thymus area.

THE LEFT LUNG

The lung area encompasses the ball of the foot, from the shoulder girdle line to the diaphragm line. Pull back the toes slightly with your right hand, with your fingers cupped over the front of the toes and your thumb at the back. Using your left thumb, caterpillar-walk in vertical strips from the diaphragm line to the shoulder girdle line on the sole of the foot. Thumb-walk until the whole of the area between the shoulder girdle line and the diaphragm line has been covered.

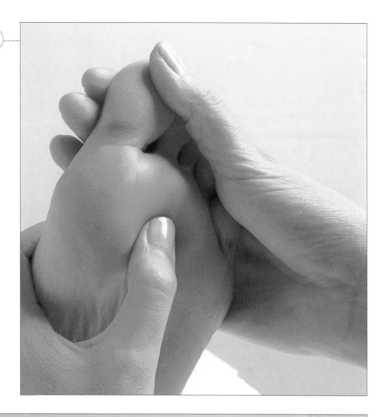

INDICATIONS

- all lung problems, such as coughs and colds
- chest infections
- asthma
- bronchitis
- emphysema
- shallow breathing
- hyperventilation and panic attacks

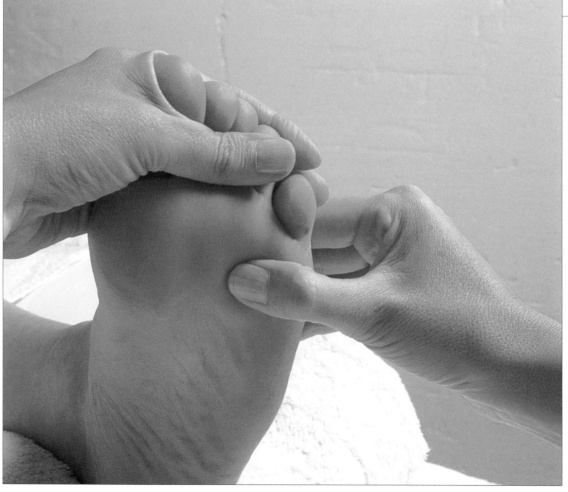

② You may also work this area by caterpillar-walking across the foot in horizontal, instead of vertical, strips.

THE LEFT BREAST/LUNGS/RIBS/MAMMARY GLANDS

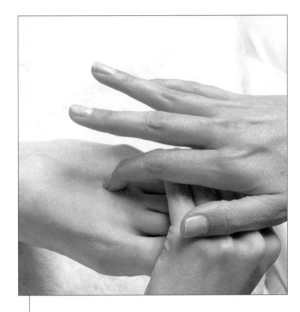

(1) Pull the toes forward with your left hand, with your thumb under the sole of the foot and your fingers cupped over the top of the toes. Finger-walk down the troughs on the top of the foot, from the base of the toes to the diaphragm line. Cover the entire area in vertical strips. As the top of the foot is more sensitive, use your index finger to do the walking.

(2) To cover the area more quickly, try using two or more fingers at once.

(3) If you wish, you may also "walk" across this area in horizontal strips.

INDICATIONS

- lung problems
- breast problems, such as tenderness due to P.M.T.
- harmless lumps that have been investigated

(4) You can also support the foot by making a fist with one of your hands and placing it under the toes as a support; now finger-walk as described earlier.

THE SHOULDER

When you treated the left lung, you were also inadvertently treating the left shoulder. The reflex for the shoulder is partly located between the shoulder girdle and the diaphragm line in zone five under the little toe. It is also found on the lateral (outer) edge at the base of the little toe.

INDICATIONS

● aches and pains in the shoulder
● stiff shoulder
● arthritis
● inflammatory conditions, such as bursitis and tendonitis

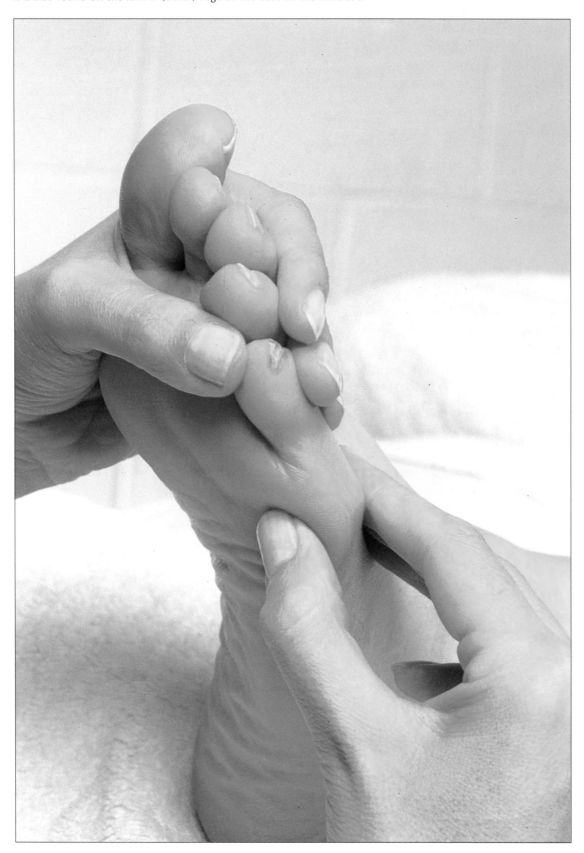

Place your thumb at the outside edge of the little toe and perform pressure circles to treat both the area under, and at the lateral edge of, the toe. This area usually needs attention, as it will often feel "gritty" and congested.

The Diaphragm Line to the Waist Line

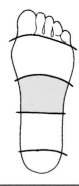

THE HEART AREA

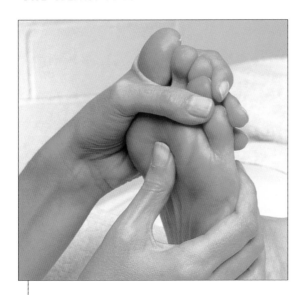

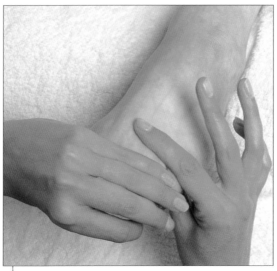

① Support the top of the foot with your left hand and wrap your right hand around it, with your thumb underneath and fingers on top. With your thumb, massage the upper third of the sole of the left foot in a circular direction.

② Pull down the toe and use your right index finger to massage the upper third of the top of the foot.

INDICATIONS

- to strengthen and regulate the heart
- palpitations
- circulatory problems
- blood-pressure problems

CAUTION

- If the receiver feels any pain in the heart area, do not apply any deeper pressure. If you are not a professional reflexologist, omit this area if the receiver has severe heart problems or a pacemaker.

THE STOMACH/PANCREAS/DUODENUM

INDICATIONS

- stomach: indigestion
- heartburn
- ulcers
- stomach cramps
- pancreas: digestive disorders
- diabetes
- hypoglycemia (low blood sugar)

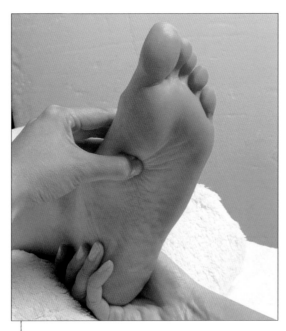

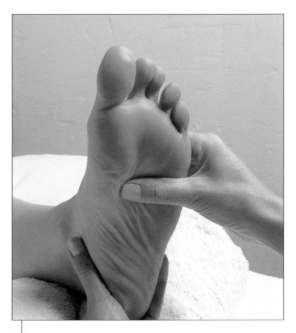

① Place your left thumb below the inside edge of the diaphragm line. Caterpillar-walk to the waist line horizontally from zones one to four.

② You may reverse your hands to work in the opposite direction if this feels more comfortable.

THE SPLEEN (LEFT FOOT ONLY)

The spleen reflex point is found only on the left foot. Support the foot with your left hand. Place your right thumb just below the diaphragm line and "walk" from zone five to zone four in horizontal rows.

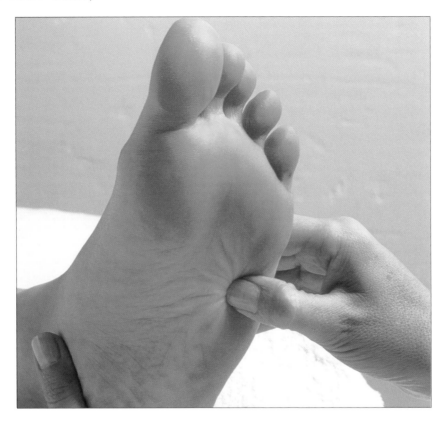

INDICATIONS

● to build up the immune system

THE ADRENAL GLAND

INDICATIONS

● all nervous disorders
● inflammatory conditions, particularly rheumatoid arthritis
● allergies, especially asthma
● lack of energy and exhaustion
● pain relief

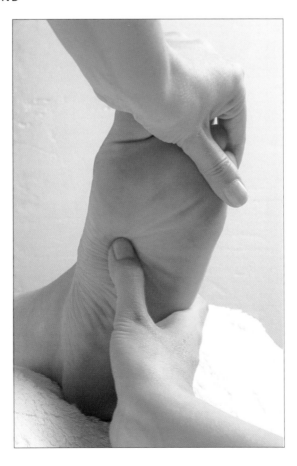

The adrenal-gland area is usually easily pinpointed as it is often tender. If you pull back the toes, a thick tendon will protrude, running from the big toe to the heel. The adrenal reflex point is located approximately midway between the diaphragm and the waist line, on the medial side (inside) of this tendon.

Hold the left foot with your left hand, with your fingers wrapped around the top of the foot. Place your right thumb on the adrenal point. Use your left hand to flex the foot on to your right thumb and rotate the foot around the thumb.

Below the Waist line

THE LEFT KIDNEY/URETER TUBE/BLADDER

INDICATIONS

- bladder infections
- cystitis
- fluid retention
- bedwetting
- incontinence
- kidney infections

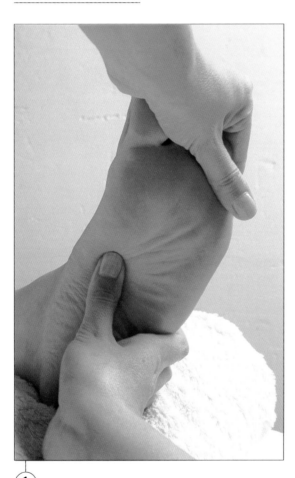

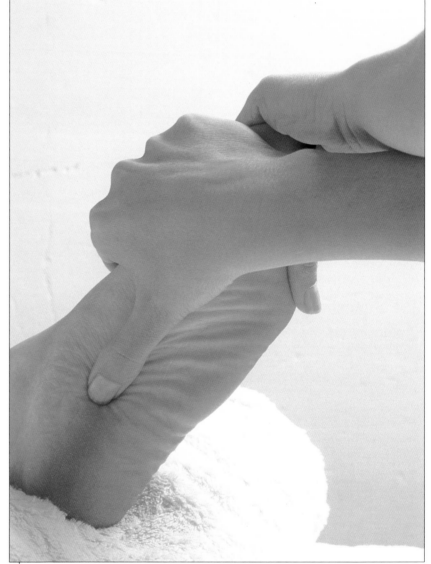

1 Part of the kidney reflex is located just above the waist line, between zones two and three. The other half of the kidney, ureter-tube, and bladder areas is located below the waist line. After you have gently rotated the adrenal reflex, move your thumb down slightly and you will have found the kidney reflex point on the waist line. With the tip of your thumb pointing toward the toes, press into the area and circle your thumb gently over it several times.

2 Turn your thumb around so that it is facing downward and then caterpillar-walk down the ureter reflex toward the inside of the foot, where the bladder reflex is situated beneath the inner ankle bone.

THE SMALL INTESTINE

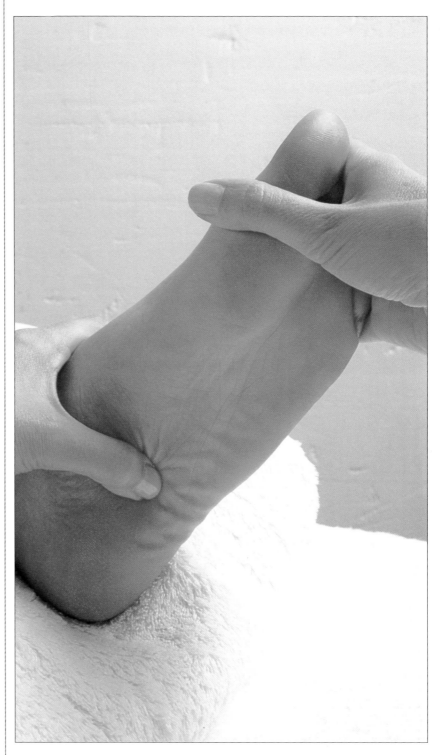

③ The bladder area can often look slightly puffy, particularly if a woman is premenstrual. Either thumb-walk over, or perform pressure circles on, the bladder reflex.

Hold back the left foot with your right hand and caterpillar-walk in horizontal rows from just below the waist line to the pelvic-floor line, from the medial aspect (inside) of the foot as far as zone four. You may work on the whole of this area in the opposite direction.

INDICATIONS

● digestive problems
● abdominal cramps

THE TRANSVERSE COLON/DESCENDING COLON/SIGMOID COLON/RECTUM AND ANUS

Hold the foot in your right hand. Place your left thumb just below the waist line on the inside of the foot.

Caterpillar-walk ① across the transverse colon, following the waist line until you reach zone three.

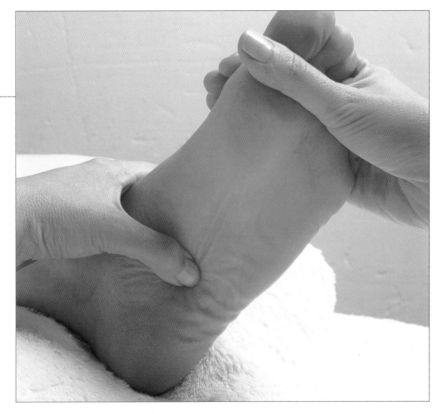

INDICATIONS

- digestive problems, such as constipation
- diarrhea
- irritable-bowel syndrome
- Crohn's disease
- ceiiac disease

Change hands and use your right thumb ② to "walk" down zone five toward the heel – this is the descending-colon area.

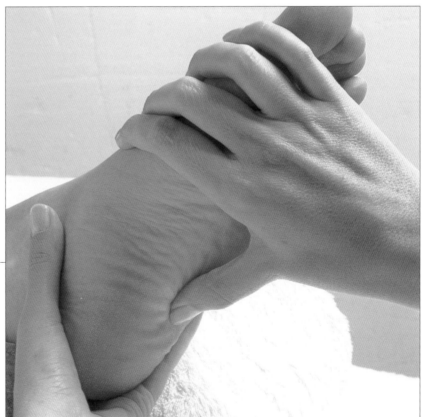

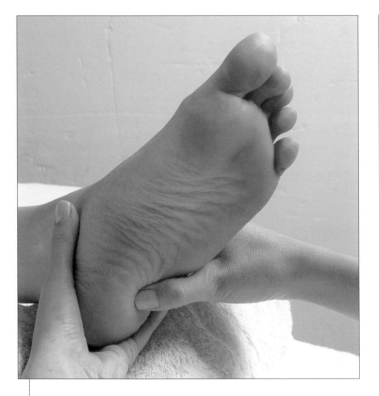

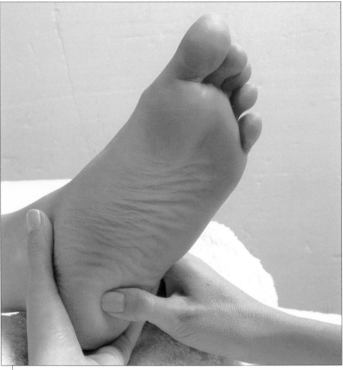

③ Just before you reach the pelvic-floor line, turn your thumb 45° diagonally to the left.

④ "Walk" to the sciatic-nerve line. Circle over this area to treat the sigmoid colon.

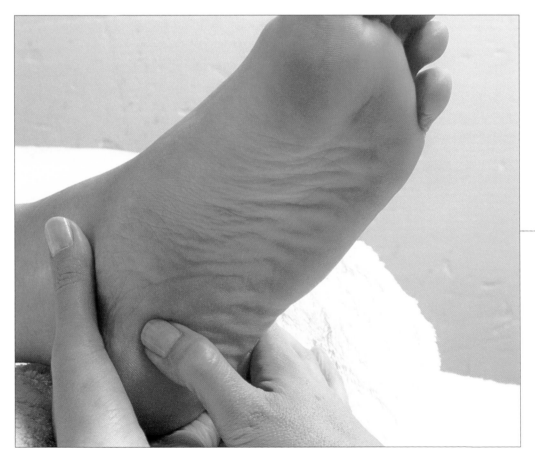

⑤ Caterpillar-walk toward the bladder area to treat the rectum and anus.

The Outer Aspect of the Foot

THE JOINTS. LEFT SHOULDER/ARM/ELBOW/HAND/HIP/KNEE AND LEG

The areas corresponding to the joints of the body are situated along the outer edge of the foot. (Remember that the spine area runs the length of the inside of the foot.)

INDICATIONS

- all joint problems, including arthritis
- sports injuries, such as tennis elbow
- stiff shoulder
- housemaid's knee
- cartilage and ligament problems

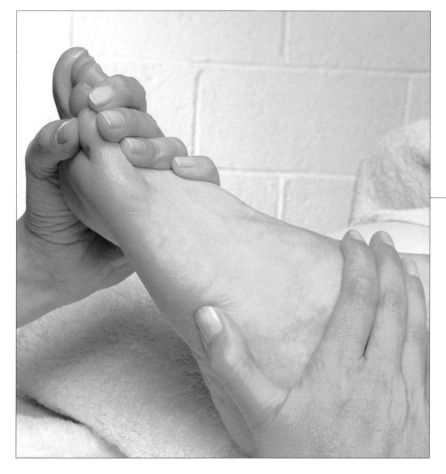

1 Hold the toes of the left foot with your left hand, and, using your right thumb, caterpillar-walk vertically up the outer edge of the foot, from the heel area up to the little toe.

2 If you wish ,you may cup the left heel with your right hand and repeat the thumb-walking in the opposite direction, from the little toe to the heel. If you come across any areas that are tender, gently circle your thumb over them several times. The shoulder reflex on the bony prominence at the base of the little toe is likely to need attention. Perform some pressure circles over this reflex.

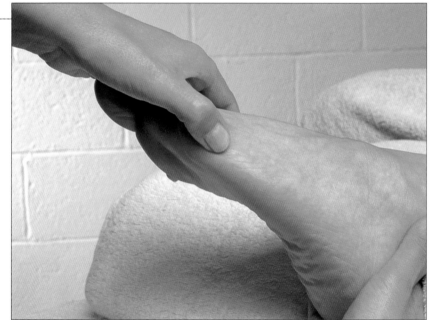

(3) The protrusion farther down, on the side of the foot, is the knee reflex. Perform several pressure circles.

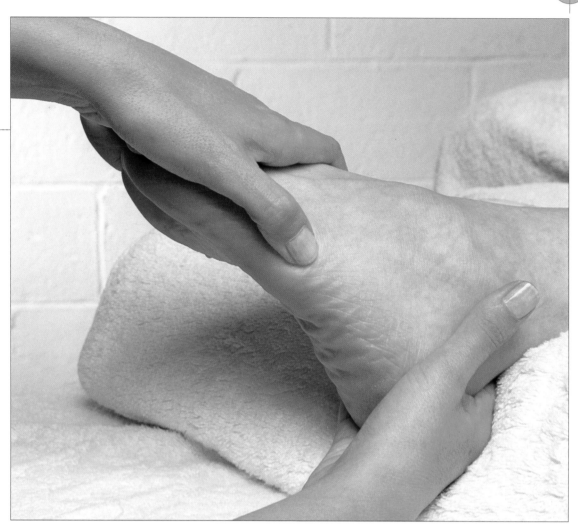

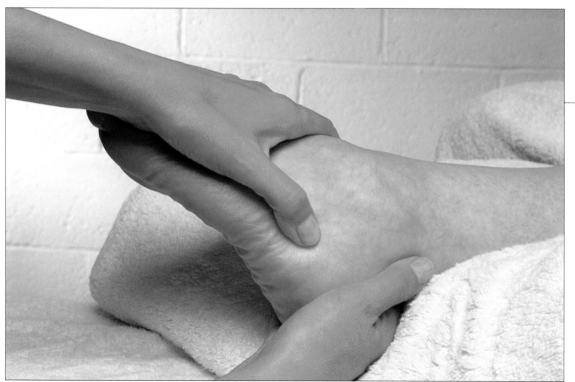

(4) Slightly farther down is the hip reflex. Perform pressure circles here, too.

Around the Ankles

THE SCIATIC-NERVE LINE/PELVIC AREA

The area around the Achilles tendon is not only worked for problems with the sciatic nerve, but also for chronic ailments related to the prostate, uterus, and rectum.

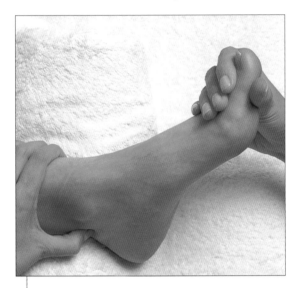

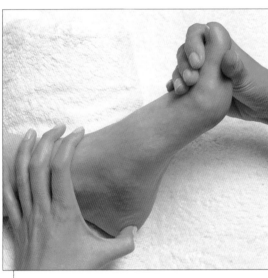

INDICATIONS

- sciatica
- lower-back and hip problems
- chronic problems with the uterus
- prostate and rectum problems

1. Hold the ball of the left foot with your right hand and place your right thumb above the inner anklebone. Now thumb-walk down the Achilles-tendon area toward the heel.

2. Continue to thumb-walk across the sciatic-nerve line on the hard heel pad of the left foot.

Finger- or 3 thumb-walk up the outside of the foot along the Achilles-tendon line, changing hands if necessary.

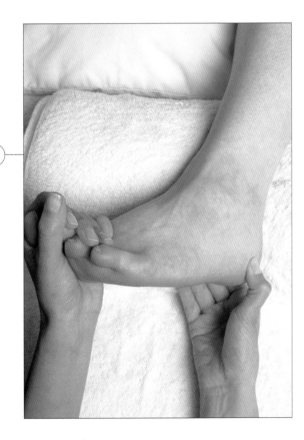

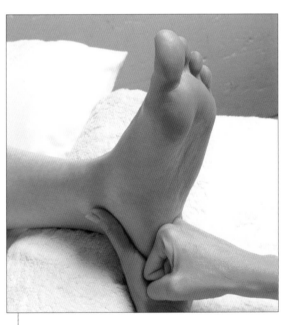

4. If the receiver has pelvic problems, work across the heel pad. Cup the foot with your left hand and gently work the area with your knuckles in a circular direction.

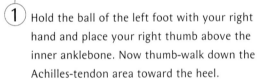

THE LEFT TESTICLE/OVARY

All of the reproductive-organ reflexes are situated around the ankle area. If the receiver is pregnant, the reproductive areas should be avoided if you are not a professional reflexologist. (A fully qualified reflexologist will use stroking movements over the uterus and ovary reflexes.)

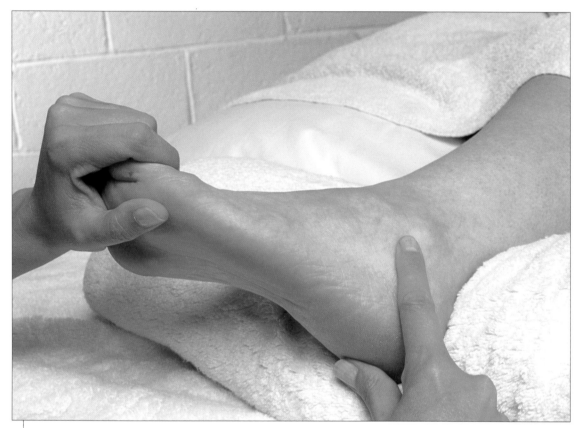

INDICATIONS

- infertility problems
- menstrual irregularities
- ovarian cysts
- the menopause

(1) Locate the testicle/ovary reflex by drawing an imaginary diagonal line from the outer anklebone to the top of the heel and then finding the midpoint.

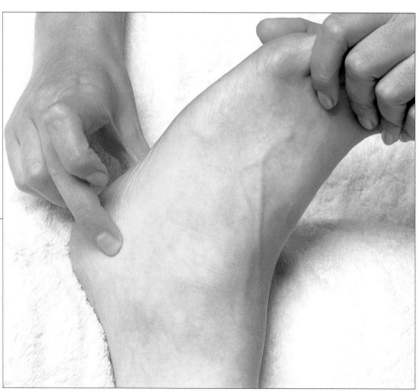

Perform small, circular movements over this area – here it is the ovary area, since the receiver is female – with your index finger. (2)

THE FALLOPIAN TUBES/VAS DEFERENS/LYMPH AND GROIN

INDICATIONS

- problems with the male or female reproductive organs
- swelling of the feet

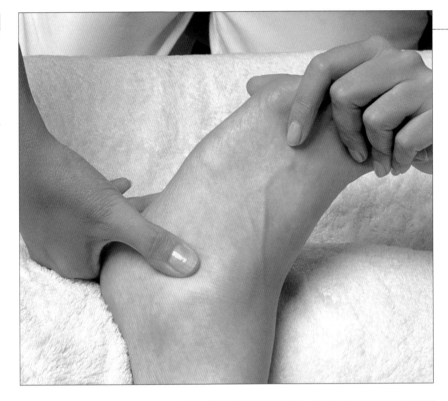

1 Using your right thumb, "walk" from the outside of the ankle across the top of the foot to the inside of the ankle. This area may be walked in both directions. The Fallopian-tube/lymph/groin reflex is illustrated here.

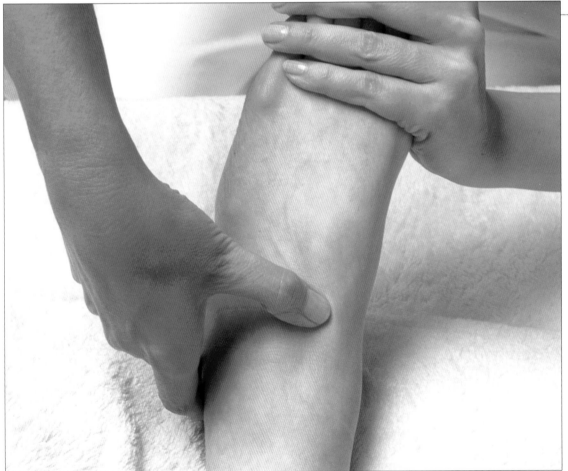

2 This can be quite a sensitive area. Remember that if you find a tender area, you should gently massage it in a circular direction. If the area is tender, it is likely to indicate a clogged-up lymphatic system. The lymphatic system is usually overburdened by poor diet, pollution, chemicals, stress, and lack of exercise.

THE PROSTATE/UTERUS

Remember to avoid this area if the receiver is pregnant and you are not a professional reflexologist.

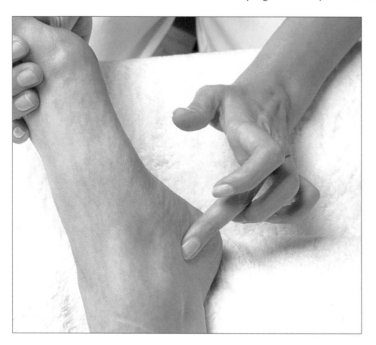

To locate the prostate/uterus point, place your index finger on the inner anklebone and your third finger on the tip of the heel. Imagine a straight line running between your fingers. The prostate/uterus point lies in the middle of this imaginary line. Here we are working on the uterus reflex. Place your index or middle finger on the point and perform small pressure circles. (These fingers are used because this is often a tender area.)

INDICATIONS

- all menstrual problems
- painful, irregular periods
- scanty or heavy periods
- fertility problems
- P.M.T.
- the menopause
- prostate problems

THE FINALE

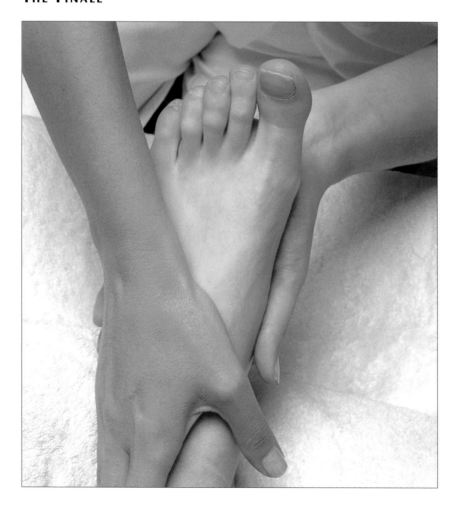

Using both hands, stroke the whole of the left foot, working from the toes, gliding around the anklebones, and then moving back again. Repeat these movements several times to ensure that any toxins that have been released during the reflexology sequence are dispersed and that the foot is totally relaxed. Now cover up the left foot.

Completing the Feet

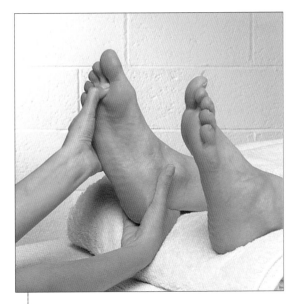

1. Uncover both feet and briefly treat any reflex points that were tender during the initial treatment. Perform a few of your favorite relaxation techniques.

2. Now perform the lower-back release. Cup your hands under the heels of both feet. Lean backward and then slowly and gently pull the feet toward you. Release the stretch very gradually.

Now perform the solar-plexus release. This technique is often used to complete a treatment. The solar plexus is the main area that stores stress and tension. Applying pressure to this area encourages a state of relaxation and also helps breathing to deepen and slow down. The solar-plexus release may be 3. performed on one or both feet.

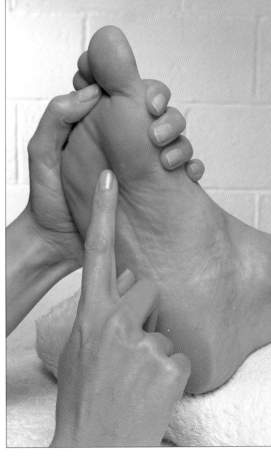

To locate the solar-plexus area, place one hand over the top of the upper part of the foot and squeeze gently. A hollow will appear on the sole of the foot at the diaphragm line. This is the solar-plexus area. Release the foot, remembering where this point is situated. Now find the solar-plexus area on the other foot.

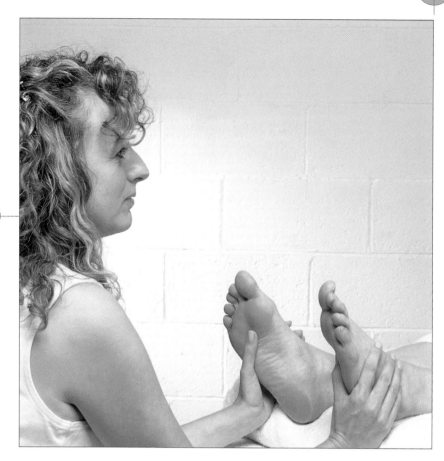

Take the left foot in your right hand and the ④ right foot in your left hand, with your fingers on top and thumbs on the bottom. Place your thumbs on the solar-plexus reflexes and press them very gently and slowly. Hold the pressure for a few seconds. Now gradually release the pressure, but do not lose contact with the feet. Repeat this procedure several times. You can synchronize this technique with the receiver's breathing. Ask them to take a deep breath, and, as they do, press into the solar-plexus areas. As they slowly breathe out, release the pressure on the points.

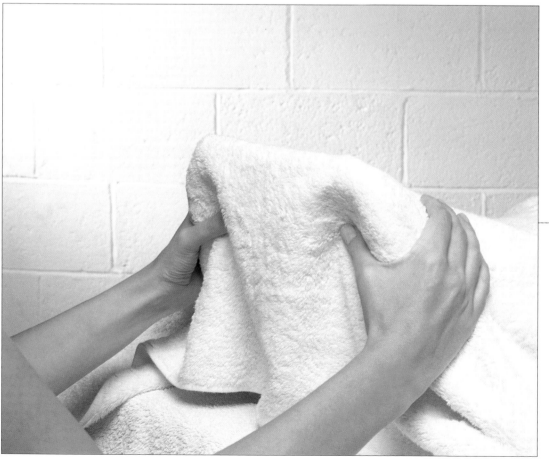

⑤ Finally, cover up the feet and ask the receiver to relax. When they get up, it is a good idea to offer them a glass of water to flush away any toxins. Encourage them to drink lots of water over the next 24 hours to assist the detoxification process.

Reflexology Charts

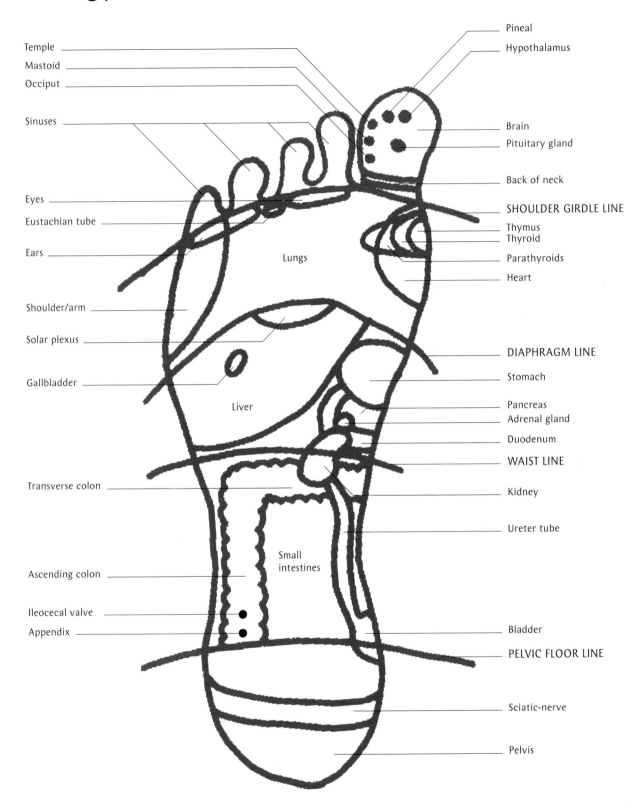

Pineal
Hypothalamus
Temple
Mastoid
Occiput
Sinuses
Brain
Pituitary gland
Back of neck
Eyes
Eustachian tube
SHOULDER GIRDLE LINE
Thymus
Thyroid
Ears
Parathyroids
Heart
Lungs
Shoulder/arm
Solar plexus
DIAPHRAGM LINE
Gallbladder
Stomach
Liver
Pancreas
Adrenal gland
Duodenum
WAIST LINE
Transverse colon
Kidney
Ureter tube
Small
intestines
Ascending colon
Ileocecal valve
Appendix
Bladder
PELVIC FLOOR LINE
Sciatic-nerve
Pelvis

RIGHT SOLE

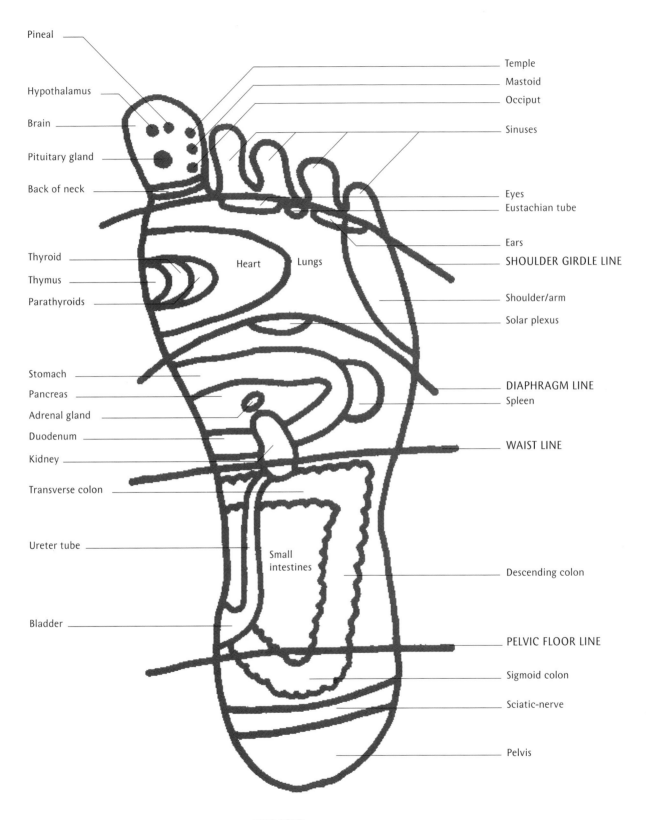

Pineal

Hypothalamus

Brain

Pituitary gland

Back of neck

Temple

Mastoid

Occiput

Sinuses

Eyes

Eustachian tube

Ears

SHOULDER GIRDLE LINE

Thyroid

Thymus

Parathyroids

Heart   Lungs

Shoulder/arm

Solar plexus

Stomach

Pancreas

Adrenal gland

Duodenum

Kidney

Transverse colon

DIAPHRAGM LINE

Spleen

WAIST LINE

Ureter tube

Small intestines

Descending colon

Bladder

PELVIC FLOOR LINE

Sigmoid colon

Sciatic-nerve

Pelvis

LEFT SOLE

Reflexology Charts (Continued)

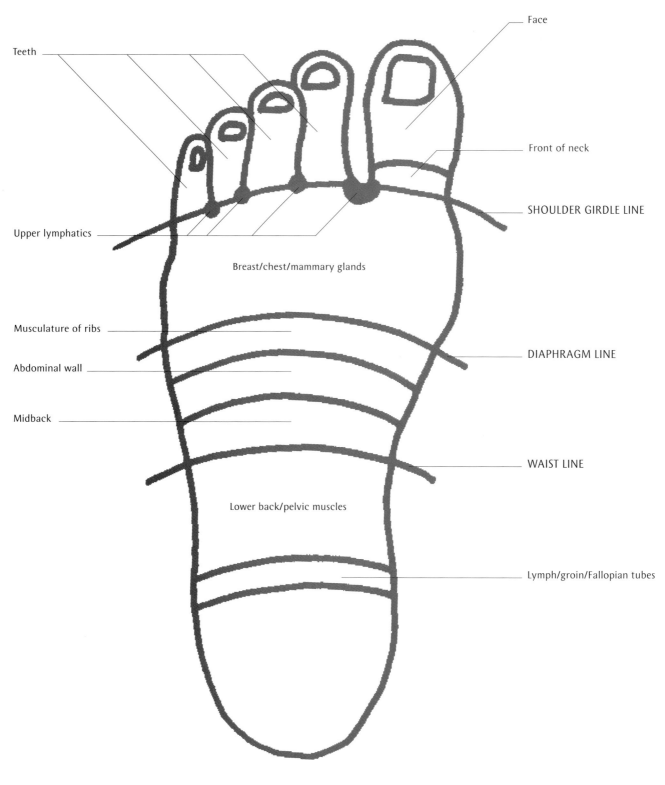

Face

Teeth

Front of neck

SHOULDER GIRDLE LINE

Upper lymphatics

Breast/chest/mammary glands

Musculature of ribs

DIAPHRAGM LINE

Abdominal wall

Midback

WAIST LINE

Lower back/pelvic muscles

Lymph/groin/Fallopian tubes

LEFT DORSUM (reflex areas on
right dorsum will be the same)

OUTSIDE VIEW OF LEFT FOOT

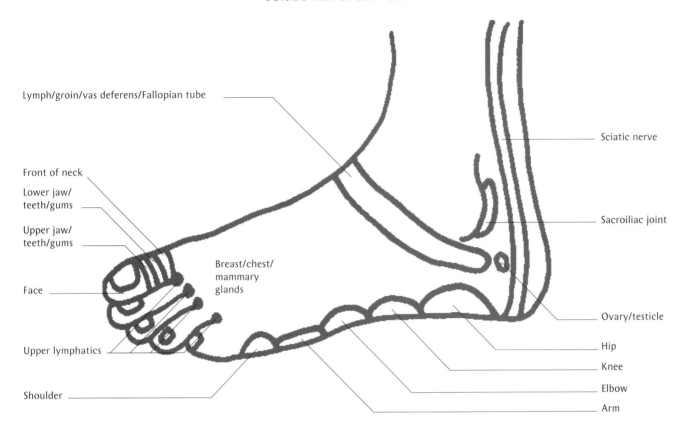

Lymph/groin/vas deferens/Fallopian tube

Front of neck

Lower jaw/
teeth/gums

Upper jaw/
teeth/gums

Face

Upper lymphatics

Shoulder

Breast/chest/
mammary
glands

Sciatic nerve

Sacroiliac joint

Ovary/testicle

Hip

Knee

Elbow

Arm

INSIDE VIEW OF LEFT FOOT

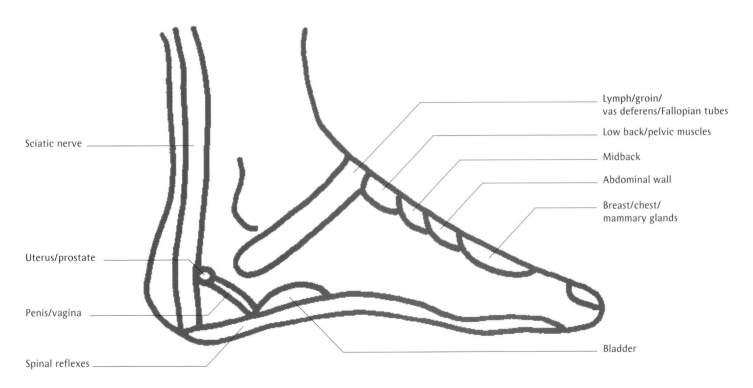

Sciatic nerve

Uterus/prostate

Penis/vagina

Spinal reflexes

Lymph/groin/
vas deferens/Fallopian tubes

Low back/pelvic muscles

Midback

Abdominal wall

Breast/chest/
mammary glands

Bladder

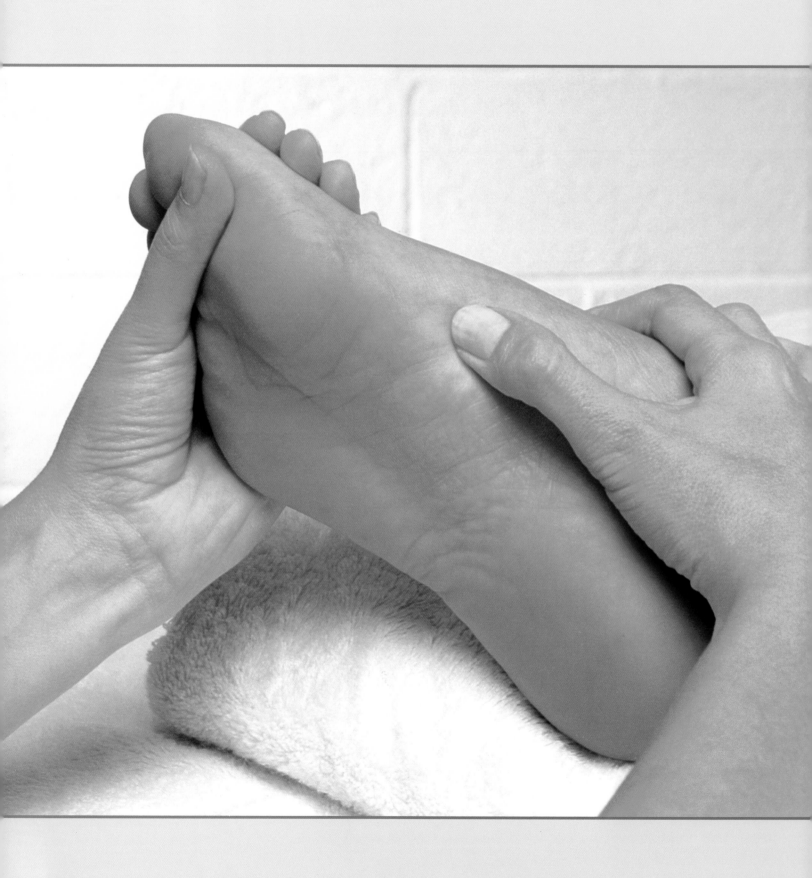

CHAPTER 6

THE SYSTEMS OF THE BODY

THE SYSTEMS OF THE BODY

Many disorders can be successfully treated using reflexology. This chapter looks at each system of the body individually. It contains a brief outline of each, the representation of each on the feet, details on how to strengthen each system, and the disorders that may benefit from their treatment, together with the relevant reflexology procedures.

The Circulatory System

The circulatory, or cardiovascular, system consists of the heart, arteries, veins, capillaries, and the blood.

The heart is a muscular pump that lies roughly in the center of the chest, behind the sternum (breastbone), two-thirds to the left and one-third to the right. It has four chambers: the right and left atria in the upper part of the heart and the right and left ventricles in the lower part. The right and left sides of the heart are separated by the septum.

The heart pumps the blood around the body via the arteries, capillaries, and veins. The right side of the heart receives deoxygenated blood and pumps it to the lungs, where the blood is reoxygenated. This freshly oxygenated blood is returned to the left-hand side of the heart and is then pumped to all parts of the body. Arteries carry blood from the heart, whereas veins carry blood to the heart.

Representation on the Feet

As the circulatory system is extensively distributed, its reflexes are found throughout the whole foot. As you massage the feet, you are improving the circulation in general.

The heart reflex is mainly found on the left foot, between the shoulder girdle line and the diaphragm line. It is also located in zone one on the right foot.

Benefits of Treatment

Treatment of this system may:
1. strengthen and regulate the heart
2. reduce palpitations
3. improve the circulation
4. balance blood pressure.

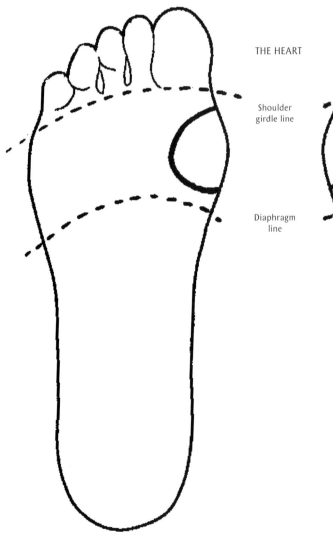

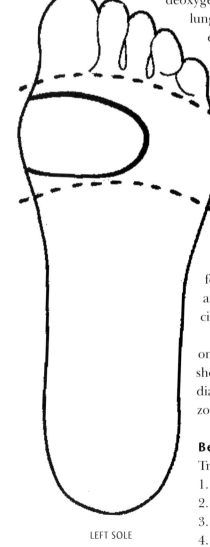

THE HEART

Shoulder girdle line

Diaphragm line

RIGHT SOLE

LEFT SOLE

Reflexology Procedure

The Left Foot Only

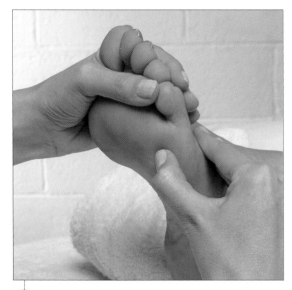

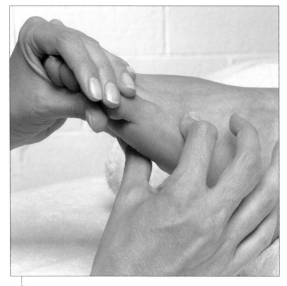

(1) Support the top of the left foot with your left hand and wrap your right hand around the foot, with your thumb underneath and fingers on top. Using your thumb, gently massage the upper third of the sole of the foot, moving in a circular direction.

(2) Pull the toes forward, and, using your right index finger, gently massage the upper third of the top of the foot.

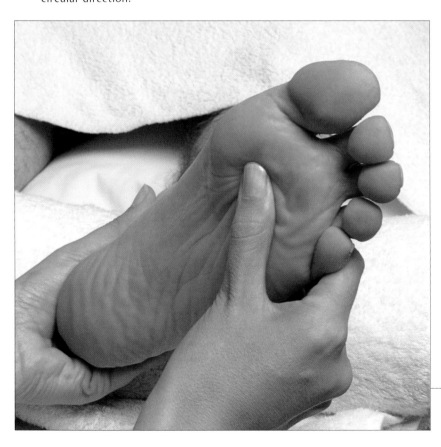

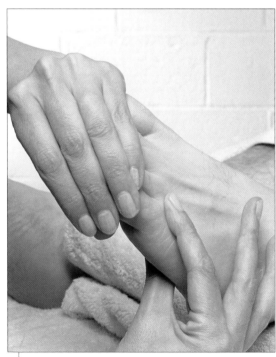

(3) Men can be particularly prone to heart problems, so a reflexology treatment covering this area can be especially beneficial for them.

The Digestive System

The digestive system begins at the mouth and descends through the thoracic and abdominal cavities to end in the anus. It is made up of the mouth, tongue, teeth, saliva glands, pharynx, esophagus, stomach, small intestine, large intestine, rectum, and anus. The pancreas, liver, and gallbladder release digestive enzymes to aid digestion.

Digestion is the process by which food is broken down into substances that the body needs for growth, repair, heat, and energy. Food is taken in (ingested) and is broken down by enzymes (digested). The digested food may then pass through the walls of certain organs into the blood and lymph to be circulated around the body (absorbed). Food substances that have been ingested, but cannot be digested or absorbed, are excreted by the bowels (eliminated).

Representation on the Feet
The reflexes of the digestive system are mostly located on the soles of the feet, between the diaphragm line and the pelvic-floor line.

Benefits of Treatment
Treatment of this system may:
1. improve the digestion, absorption, and elimination of food
2. alleviate difficulties with swallowing
3. counteract acidity, indigestion, ulcers, and s tomach cramps
4. detoxify the body
5. balance blood sugar
6. relieve constipation, diarrhea, irritable-bowel syndrome, Crohn's disease, amd celiac disease.
7. Reduce hemorrhoids.

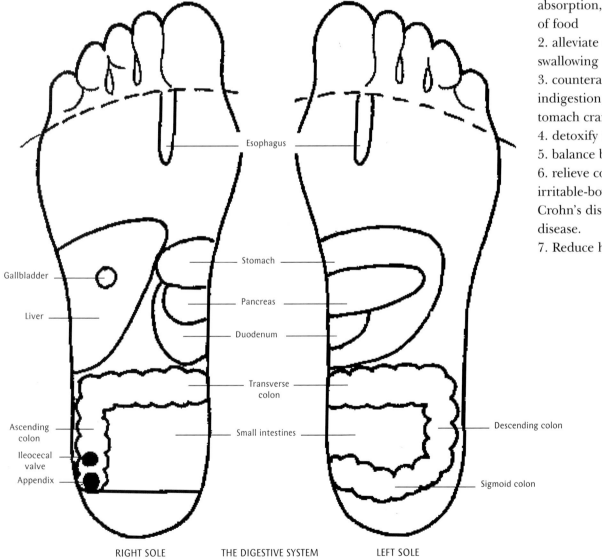

Esophagus

Gallbladder

Liver

Stomach

Pancreas

Duodenum

Transverse colon

Ascending colon

Ileocecal valve

Appendix

Small intestines

Descending colon

Sigmoid colon

RIGHT SOLE   THE DIGESTIVE SYSTEM   LEFT SOLE

Reflexology Procedure

For optimum effect, the entire digestive system should be treated.

The Right Foot

THE ESOPHAGUS

The esophagus transports food from the mouth to the stomach. The main reflex is found on the sole of the foot, in a vertical band between the first and second toes.

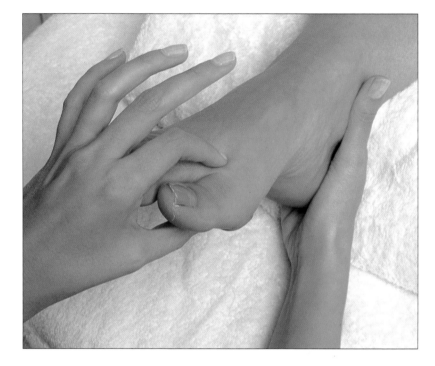

Support the foot, and, with your thumb on the bottom and index finger on the top, "walk" vertically down the foot. Start between the webbing of the first and second toes and finish at the diaphragm line.

THE LIVER/GALLBLADDER

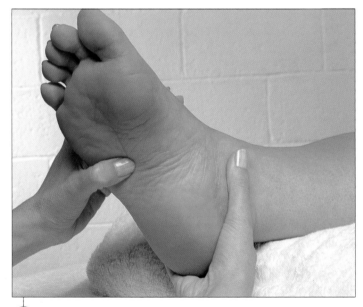

(1) To treat the liver, caterpillar-walk along the sole of the foot from zone five to zone three, between the diaphragm line and the waist line.

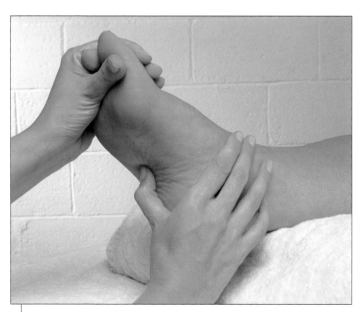

(2) Locate the gallbladder reflex, which is situated in line with the fourth toe, and then use the rotation technique. Place your thumb on the gallbladder reflex and use your holding hand to rotate the foot in a circular motion around the thumb.

THE STOMACH/PANCREAS AND DUODENUM

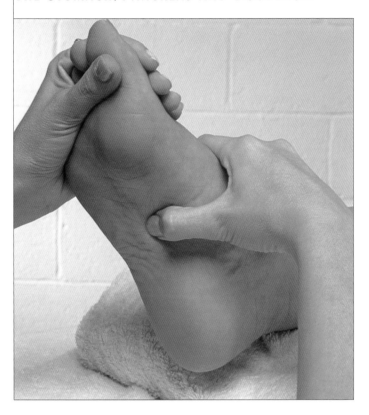

Use your left hand to hold the foot, and, with your right thumb, caterpillar-walk between the diaphragm line and the waist line from zone one to zone three.

THE SMALL INTESTINE

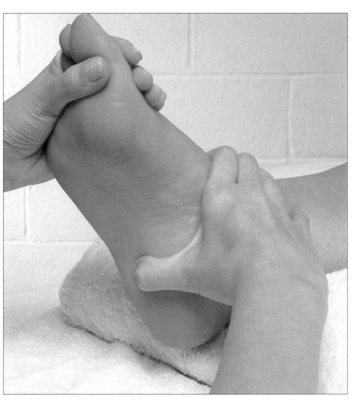

Hold the foot with your left hand and caterpillar-walk in horizontal rows from zone one to zone four, from just below the waist line to the pelvic-floor line.

THE APPENDIX/ILEOCECAL VALVE AND ASCENDING AND TRANSVERSE COLONS

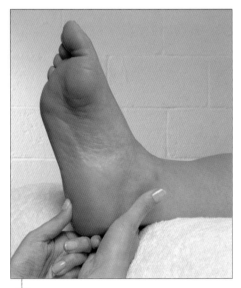

① Place your left thumb just above the pelvic-floor line in zones four and five and circle over this area to treat the appendix and ileocecal valve.

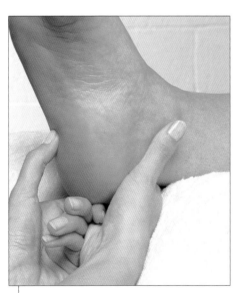

② Caterpillar-walk up the ascending-colon area in zones four and five until you reach just below the waist line.

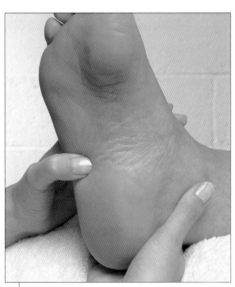

③ Turn your left thumb 90° and "walk" horizontally to the right, following the waist line across the foot, to treat the transverse colon.

The Left Foot

THE ESOPHAGUS

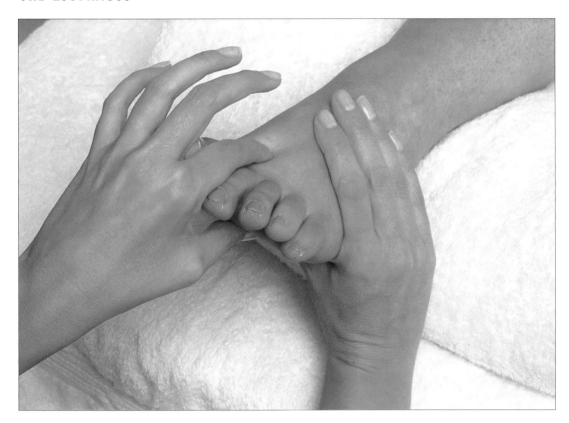

Commence at the webbing between the first and second toe. Using your thumb and index finger, "walk" straight down the foot until you reach the diaphragm line.

THE STOMACH/PANCREAS AND DUODENUM

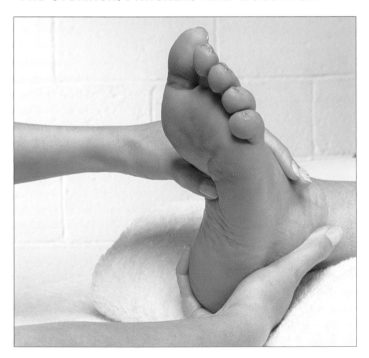

Place your left thumb just below the diaphragm line and caterpillar-walk in horizontal rows from zone one to zone four until you reach the waist line.

THE SMALL INTESTINE

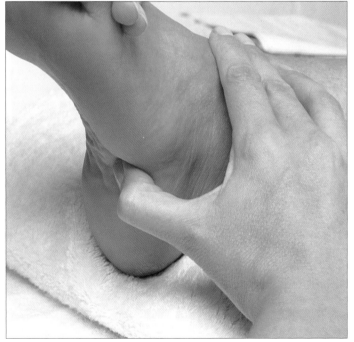

With your thumb, caterpillar-walk in horizontal rows from just below the waist line to the pelvic-floor line.

THE TRANSVERSE COLON/DESCENDING COLON/SIGMOID COLON/RECTUM AND ANUS

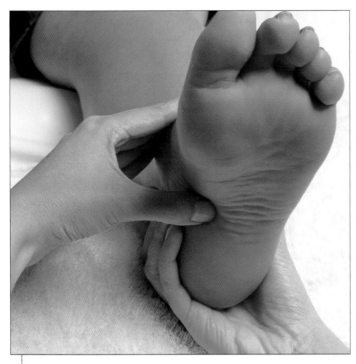

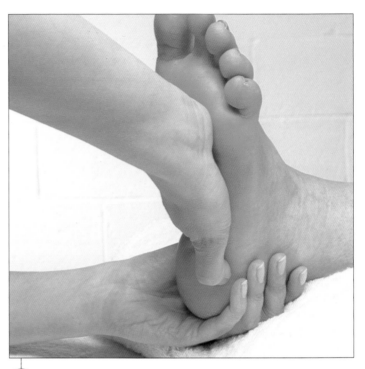

1 Place your left thumb just below the waist line in zone one and caterpillar-walk across the transverse-colon area until you reach zone five.

2 Change hands and "walk" down zone five toward the heel to treat the descending colon.

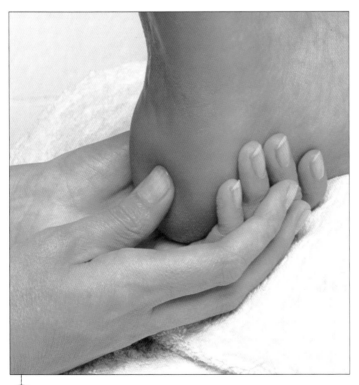

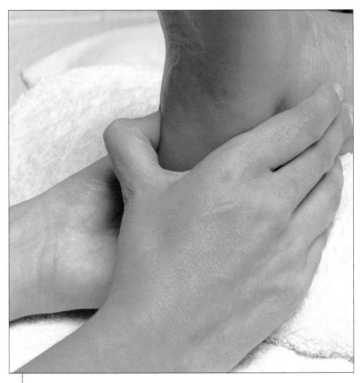

3 Just before you reach the pelvic-floor line, turn your thumb 45° diagonally to the left and "walk" down to the sciatic-nerve line. Circle over this area to treat the sigmoid colon.

4 Finally, caterpillar-walk toward the bladder area to treat the rectum and anus.

The Endocrine System

The endocrine system consists of a number of glands that are widely distributed throughout the body but have no anatomical connection.

The endocrine glands are ductless glands, because the hormones that they secrete do not pass down ducts, but directly into the bloodstream instead. Hormones are complex chemical substances that travel around the body via the bloodstream, which carries them to their target organ or tissue, where they influence activity in the appropriate way.

The endocrine glands include:

- the pituitary (one)
- the thyroid (one)
- the parathyroids (four)
- the adrenals (two)
- the thymus (one)
- the islets of Langerhans
- the pineal (one)
- the ovaries in the female body (two)
- the testes in the male body (two).

The pituitary gland, which is the size of a pea, is often described as the "master gland," or the "leader of the endocrine orchestra," as it regulates the activity of many of the other endocrine glands. It works together with the hypothalamus. The hormones secreted by the pituitary gland affect growth, stimulate uterine contractions during birth, assist breast-feeding, and perform many other functions.

The thyroid gland affects metabolism. Undersecretion of thyroxin leads to a low metabolic rate, with such symptoms as lethargy, depression, weight problems, and stunted growth in children. Overactivity leads to nervousness, an inability to relax, and thinness, despite eating lots of food.

The parathyroid glands help to balance levels of calcium and phosphorus in the blood.

The adrenal glands are situated on top of each kidney. The adrenal medulla produces adrenalin, which prepares the body to deal with such responses as fear, excitement, or anger. The adrenal cortex produces a number of hormones, including corticosteroids, that help to combat inflammation and allergies.

The thymus gland plays an important part in the immune function, while the islets of Langerhans in the pancreas help to regulate blood-sugar levels.

The pineal gland is thought to regulate the body's natural rhythms and is associated with S.A.D. (seasonal affective disorder).

The ovaries and testes will be described in the section on the reproductive system.

Representation on the Feet

The endocrine system is widely distributed throughout the feet. The reflexes are mostly found on the back of the big toe and the ball of the foot.

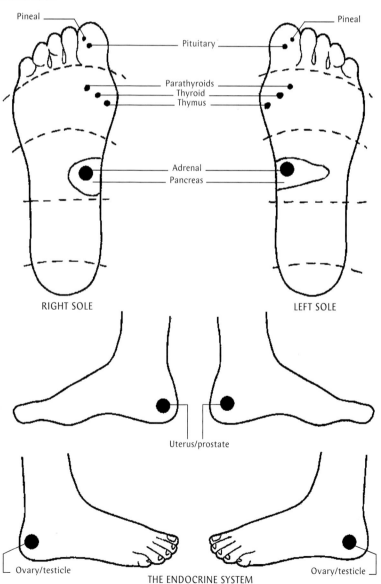

THE ENDOCRINE SYSTEM

Reflexology Procedure

The Right Foot

THE PITUITARY GLAND

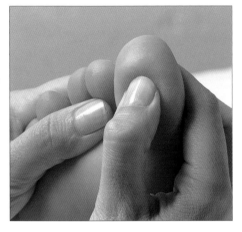

Place the fingers of your left hand over the front of the toes and your thumb under the back of the toes. Locate the widest point of the big toe, and the pituitary-gland area should be approximately at the midpoint. Use the corner of your right thumb to hook in and back up on the pituitary-gland reflex. Alternatively, you may perform pressure circles.

THE HYPOTHALAMUS/PINEAL GLAND

(1) Move your thumb slightly upward from the pituitary-gland area and perform pressure circles on the hypothalamus reflex point.

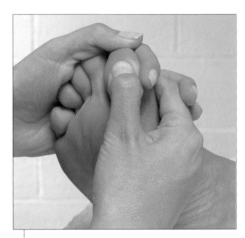

(2) Now rock your thumb on to its outer edge to circle gently over the pineal-gland area. The hypothalamus and the pineal gland should both be treated, because they work together as a unit.

THE THYROID/PARATHYROIDS AND THYMUS

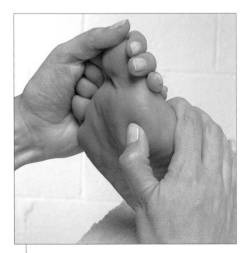

(1) To treat the thyroid, place the flat pad of your thumb in the center of the pad of the ball of the foot and perform pressure circles.

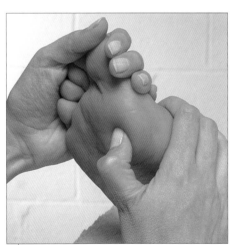

(2) Move your thumb slightly to the left and then up. Now perform pressure circles to treat the parathyroids.

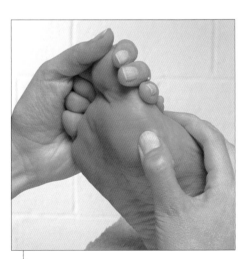

(3) Slide your thumb to the right of the thyroid-gland area and very slightly down, close to the spinal reflexes, and circle over the thymus area.

THE ADRENAL GLAND

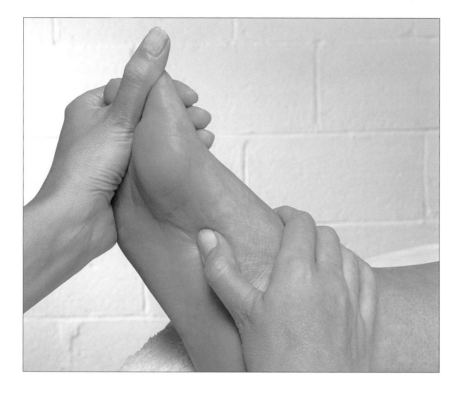

Pull back the toes and observe the thick tendon that runs from the big toe to the heel. The adrenal reflex point is located approximately midway between the diaphragm line and the waistl ine, on the medial side (inside) of this tendon.

With your left hand holding the right foot, and your fingers wrapped around the top of the foot, place your right thumb on the adrenal point. Use your left hand to flex the foot on to your right thumb and then rotate the foot around it.

THE PANCREAS

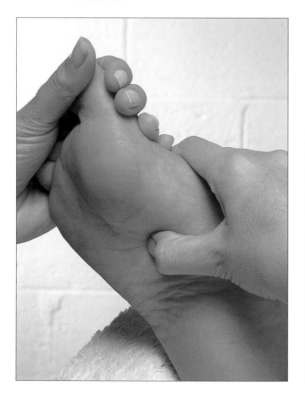

Using your left hand to hold the foot, thumb-walk from zone one to zone two, working from just below the diaphragm line to the waist line.

THE SEX GLANDS (OVARIES AND TESTES)

Details of how to treat the sex glands can be found in the section on the reproductive system.on page 119.

The Left Foot

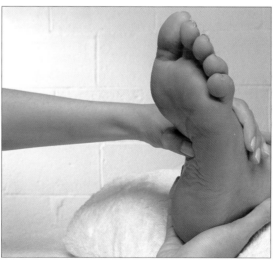

The left foot should also be treated. When working on the pancreas area, caterpillar-walk from zone one to zone three.

The Lymphatic System

The lymphatic system is widely distributed throughout the body, and can be likened to an extensive sewage network. It neutralizes and drains away excess tissue fluid and harmful wastes and toxins and plays a vital role in the body's defense and immune system.

Lymph nodes purify the lymph to prevent infection from passing into the bloodstream. The main sites of the lymph nodes are the throat, armpits, groin, abdomen, and behind the knees.

The spleen, thymus, tonsils, and appendix are also part of the lymphatic system.

Representation on the Feet

Because the lymphatic system is so widely distributed, you are having a positive effect on it even when you are only performing relaxation techniques.

The upper lymph-node areas for the neck are found between the webbing of the toes. The lymph reflexes for the groin are located on the top of the foot, from the inner to the outer anklebones. The reflexes of the axillary lymph nodes (in the armpit) can be found close to the shoulder reflex, at the base of the little toe.

Benefits of Treatment

Treatment of the lymphatic system may:

1. help to protect the body from disease by building up the body's defenses to prevent diseases from occurring
2. rid the body of excess fluid
3. shorten the recovery time from an illness.

THE LYMPHATIC SYSTEM

Upper lymph nodes
Thymus
Lower/pelvic/inguinal lymph nodes
Axillary lymph nodes
Axillary lymph nodes
Upper lymph nodes
R. DORSUM
L. DORSUM
Upper lymph nodes
R.
L.
Inner aspect
Outer aspect
Lower/pelvic/inguinal lymph nodes

Reflexology Procedure

The Right Foot
THE UPPER LYMPH NODES

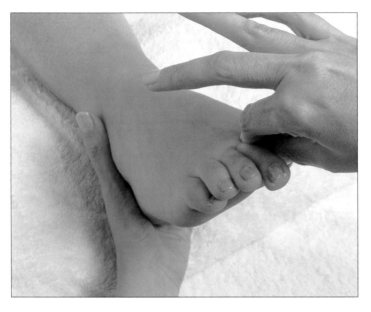

Support the right foot with your left hand. Using the thumb and index finger of your right hand, very gently squeeze the webbing between each of the toes.

THE AXILLARY LYMPH NODES

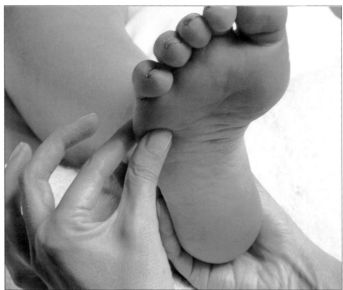

Place the index finger of your left hand on the top of the foot and your thumb on the sole of the foot, just below the shoulder reflex. Now perform several pressure circles.

THE LOWER/INGUINAL LYMPHATICS (GROIN)

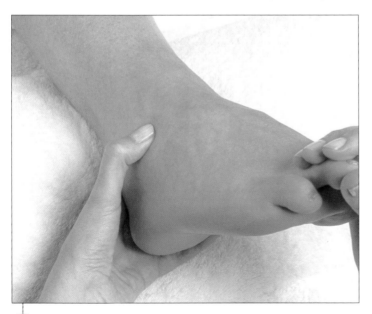

(1) Thumb- or finger-walk from the outside of the ankle across the top of the foot to the inside of the ankle. "Walk" across this area in both directions.

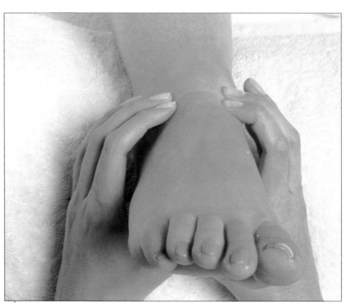

(2) An alternative method is to place both thumbs on the sole of the foot and to work over the top of the foot with the index finger, or index and middle fingers, of both hands.

Repeat *all* of the above techniques on the left foot.

The Musculoskeletal System

This system covers all of the bones and joints and the muscles that move them. Bones are linked together by ligaments, and muscles are attached to the bones by tendons.

The spine, or vertebral column, is made up of 26 vertebrae, arranged as follows:
- cervical vertebrae (seven)
- thoracic vertebrae (twelve)
- lumbar vertebrae (five)
- sacrum (one – five fused together)
- coccyx (one – four fused together).

Between the vertebrae are disks, which act as shock-absorbers for the spine. These are unfortunately subject to wear and tear and pain and stiffness, and reduced flexibility in the back is common as we grow older.

There are twelve pairs of ribs which, together with the sternum, form the ribcage. The first seven pairs of ribs are known as "true ribs," while the next five pairs are "false ribs." The eleventh and twelfth pairs are referred to as "floating ribs," since they are not attached to the sternum.

The joints of the body are susceptible to wear and tear and injuries. Some of the most commonly affected include the hip, knee, ankle, shoulder, elbow, and ankle joints.

Representation on the Feet
The spinal reflexes are located on the medial aspect of both feet.

The reflexes of the joints are found along the outer edge of both feet.

Benefits of Treatment
Treatment of this system will:
1. relax the muscles
2. restore mobility
3. relieve aches and pains
4. improve coordination
5. alleviate arthritis
6. relieve stress and tension
7. reduce sciatica
8. help repetitive-strain injuries.

MUSCULOSKELETAL SYSTEM

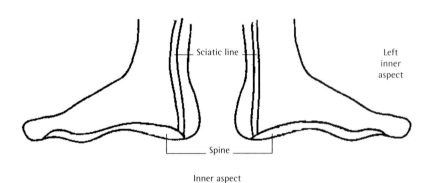

Inner aspect

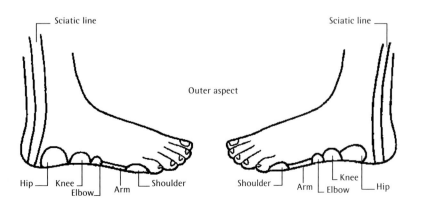

Outer aspect

Reflexology Procedure

The Right Foot

THE SPINE

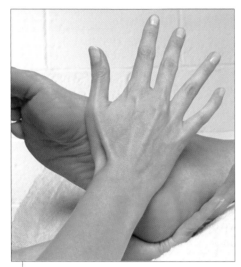

1 To relax the spine, support the foot in the palm of your holding hand and stroke down the inside of the foot with the heel of your working hand.

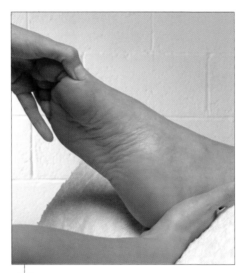

2 Support the foot under the heel with your holding hand and caterpillar-walk down the inside of the foot, beginning at the base of the toenail. This represents the top of the spine (the cervical area).

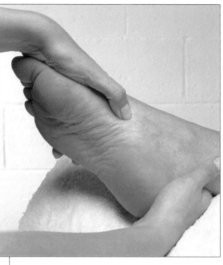

3 As you "walk" down the foot, you are covering the middle of the back (the thoracic area).

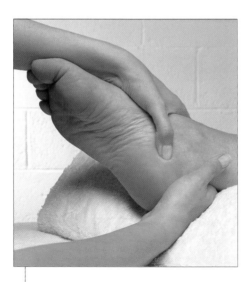

4 At the bottom of the foot, you are covering the lower back (the lumbar area).

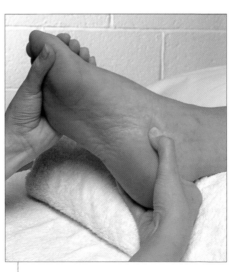

5 Now change hands. Place your holding hand at the top of the foot, with your thumb on the back of the toes and your fingers wrapped around the front of the toes.

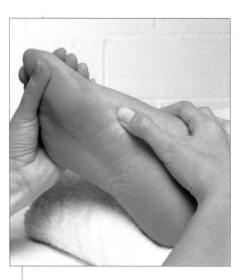

6 Working in the opposite direction, repeat the thumb-walking procedure from the base of the heel to the base of the toenail. Repeat this procedure on the other foot.

THE JOINTS

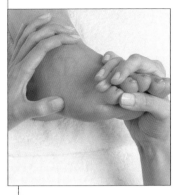

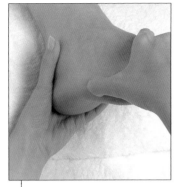

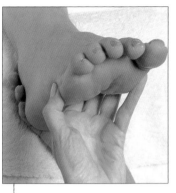

1 To give a general treatment, hold the toes of the right foot with your right hand. Use your left thumb to caterpillar-walk up the outer edge of the foot, from the heel area to the little toe.

2 Now cup the right heel with your left hand and repeat the thumb-walking procedure in the opposite direction, from the little toe to the heel.

If you are dealing with a specific joint problem, look at the diagram to find the reflex point and then perform pressure circles over it.

3 For example, to treat a stiff or painful shoulder, use pressure circles over the bony prominence at the base of the little toe.

4 If you are treating a tennis elbow, perform pressure circles a few steps below the shoulder reflex.

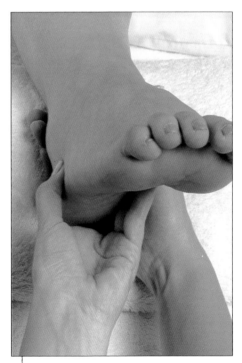

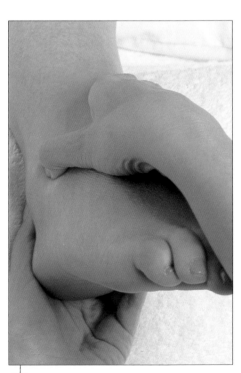

5 To treat the knee, work around the protrusion on the side of the foot.

6 To treat the hip, work approximately halfway between the knee reflex and the back of the heel.

7 The sacroiliac joint (where the sacrum meets the pelvis) can be located just in front of the anklebone, and is often felt as a small dip.

Repeat on the other foot.

THE SCIATIC-NERVE LINE/PELVIC AREA

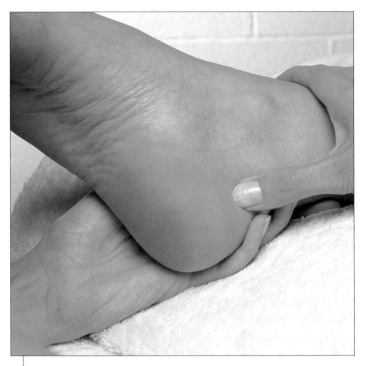

1 Hold the right foot with your left hand and place your right thumb approximately 15cm (6") above the inner anklebone. Thumb-walk down the Achilles-tendon area toward the heel.

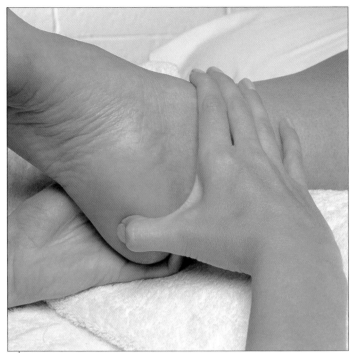

2 Continue to thumb-walk across the sciatic-nerve line on the hard heel pad of the right foot.

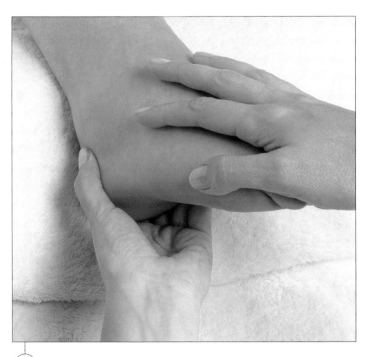

3 Finger- or thumb-walk up the outside of the foot, along the Achilles-tendon line, changing hands if necessary.

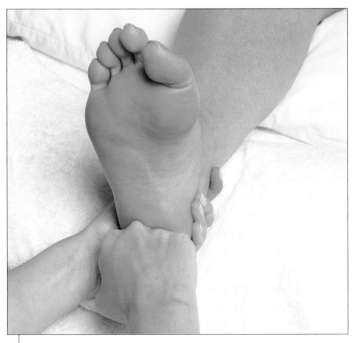

4 When the receiver has pelvic problems, it is very effective to work across the heel pad. Cup the foot with your left hand and gently work the area with your knuckles, moving in a circular direction.

Treatment of this area is particularly useful for sciatica, lower-back, and pelvic problems. Repeat on the other foot.

The Reproductive System

The reproductive system consists of the ovaries/testes, the uterus/prostate, the vagina/penis, and the Fallopian tubes/ vas deferens.

The two ovaries, one located on each side of the uterus, are the female gonads (sex glands), and are small, almond-shaped glands about 2 to 3cm (¾ to 1½") long. They produce ova (eggs), as well as the hormones estrogen and progesterone. The uterus, which is found in the pelvic cavity, is a hollow, pear-shaped organ approximately 10cm (4") long. It protects and nourishes the fetus during pregnancy. The Fallopian tubes, which are about 10 to 14cm (4 to 5½") long, connect the ovaries with the uterus. The ova, released during ovulation from the ovaries, travel down this tube to the uterus.

The two testes, which are found outside the body in the scrotum, are the male gonads. They produce spermatozoa and testosterone.

The prostate gland is situated at the base of the bladder and surrounds the urethra. The lubricating fluid that it produces forms part of the semen and helps to transport sperm cells. The vas deferens conducts semen from the prostate to the urethra.

Representation on the Feet

The ovaries/testes are represented on both feet on the outside, midway between the anklebone and the back of the heel.

The uterus/prostate reflex points are located on both feet on the inside of the ankles, midway between the anklebone and the heel.

The Fallopian tubes/vas deferens areas are found on both feet, stretching across the top of the foot from one anklebone to the other. They link the ovaries/uterus or the vas deferens/prostate.

Benefits of Treatment

Treatments of this system may:
1. regulate menstruation
2. alleviate P.M.T.
3. help with the changes of the menopause
4. increase fertility
5. relieve prostate problems
6. alleviate many of the common problems experienced in pregnancy and assist with the process of labor.

THE REPRODUCTIVE SYSTEM

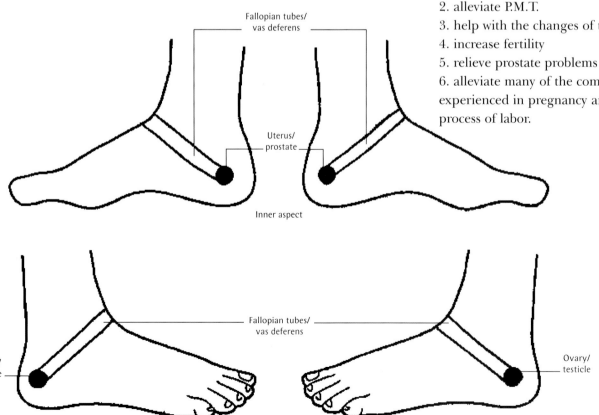

Fallopian tubes/ vas deferens

Uterus/ prostate

Inner aspect

Fallopian tubes/ vas deferens

Ovary/ testicle

Ovary/ testicle

Outer aspect

Reflexology Procedure

The Female Reproductive System (Right Foot)

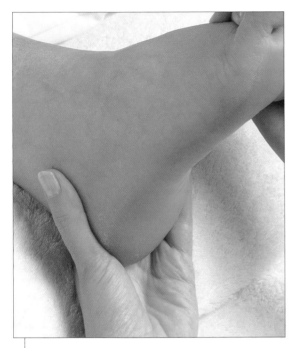

1 Locate the ovary reflex by drawing an imaginary diagonal line from the outer anklebone to the heel. The midpoint is the ovary.

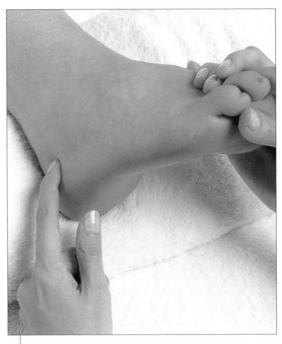

2 Use your index finger to perform small, circular movements over this reflex.

CAUTION

- if you are not a professional reflexologist, avoid the reproductive areas if the receiver is pregnant, particularly during the first three months if there is a history of miscarriage

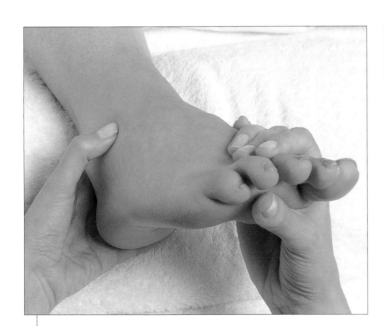

3 Thumb- or finger-walk across the Fallopian-tube area, from the ovary reflex point on the outside of the ankle to the uterus point on the inside of the ankle.

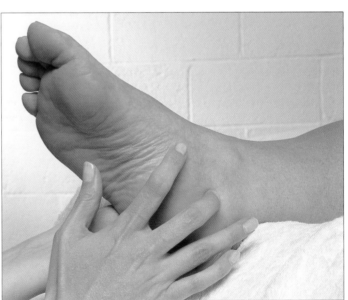

4 The uterus reflex point is also found midway between the anklebone and the heel. Perform small pressure circles over this area with the index finger.
Repeat on the other foot.

The Male Reproductive System

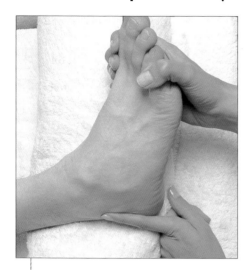

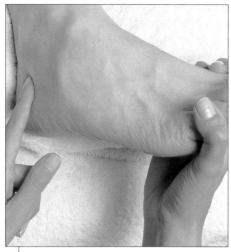

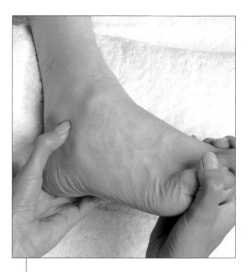

(1) Locate the testicle reflex by drawing an imaginary diagonal line from the outer anklebone to the heel. The midpoint is the testicle reflex.

(2) Use your index finger to perform small circular movements over this reflex.

(3) Thumb- or finger-walk across the vas deferens area, from the testicle point on the outside of the ankle to the prostate area on the inside.

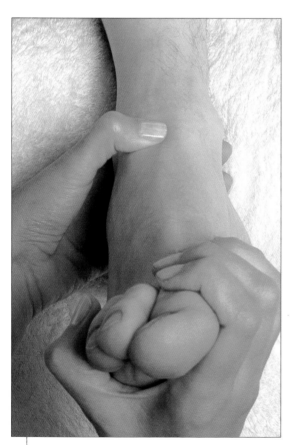

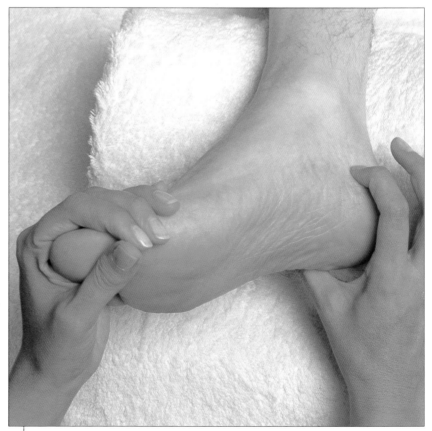

(4) Continue thumb- or finger-walking over the foot until you reach the prostate area on the inside of the ankle.

(5) The prostate is found midway between the anklebone and the heel. Perform small pressure circles with the index finger over this area.
Repeat on the other foot.

The Respiratory System

The respiratory system is concerned with breathing and consists of two tracts: the upper respiratory tract, which includes the nasal passages, the pharynx, and larynx, and the lower respiratory tract, which includes the trachea (windpipe), bronchi, lungs, and diaphragm.

Air is breathed in through the nose, where it is warmed, moistened, and filtered. It passes through the pharynx (the throat) and larynx (the voicebox) into the trachea (the windpipe). The trachea divides into two bronchi, which take air into the lungs. Each bronchus divides into smaller tubes, called bronchioles. At the end of the bronchioles are alveoli (tiny air sacs), surrounded by capillaries, through which the exchange of gases takes place. The oxygen is taken up by the blood and the carbon dioxide is taken up into the air sacs to be breathed out. The two lungs are enclosed by the ribs and the diaphragm.

Representation on the Feet

The reflexes of the respiratory system are found in both feet, on the upper and lower surfaces between the shoulder girdle line and the diaphragm line.

Benefits of Treatment

Treatment of this system may:
1. help breathing to deepen, become regulated, and slow down
2. clear congestion and mucus
3. accelerate recovery from, and prevent, coughs, colds, and chest infections
4. relieve asthma
5. alleviate inflammation,e.g., bronchitis.
6. decrease panic attacks and hyperventilation.

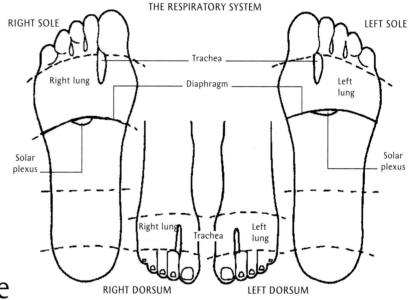

THE RESPIRATORY SYSTEM

RIGHT SOLE — Trachea — Right lung — Solar plexus

LEFT SOLE — Trachea — Left lung — Solar plexus — Diaphragm

Right lung — Trachea — Left lung

RIGHT DORSUM — LEFT DORSUM

Reflexology Procedure

The Right Foot

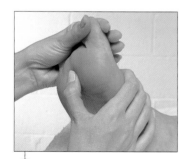

① Support the right foot with your left hand and pull back the toes slightly. Caterpillar-walk upward in vertical strips from the diaphragm line to the shoulder girdle line.

② If you prefer, you may "walk" across the foot in horizontal strips.

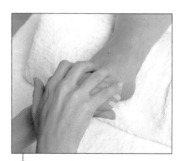

③ Now pull the toes forward and finger-walk (because the dorsum of the foot is more sensitive) down the top of the foot, from the base of the toes to the diaphragm line.

④ Once again, if you wish, you may "walk" this area in horizontal strips.
Repeat these steps on the left foot.

The Urinary System

The urinary system is composed of two kidneys, two ureter tubes, the bladder, and the urethra. The kidneys are two bean-shaped organs, the left one a little higher than the right, found slightly above the waist on either side of the spine. They act as a filtering system for the blood, removing any waste products that are excreted as liquid urine. The ureters carry the urine from the kidneys to the bladder, where it passes out of the urethra. About 1.5 liters (2 1/2 pints) of urine are excreted daily. (It is estimated that the kidneys process approximately 150 to 190 liters – 33 to 42 gallons – of fluid each day.)

Representation on the Feet

The kidneys are reflected on the soles of both feet. Part of the kidney area is located just above the waist line, between zones two and three. The other half of the kidney area is located below the waist line. The ureter reflex extends from the kidney area to the bladder reflex, that is, the often slightly swollen area at the base of the instep.

Benefits of Treatment

Treatment of this system may:
1. relieve cystitis
2. help kidney infections
3. ease renal colic
4. alleviate fluid retention
5. normalize bladder action, e.g., help incontinence.

THE URINARY SYSTEM

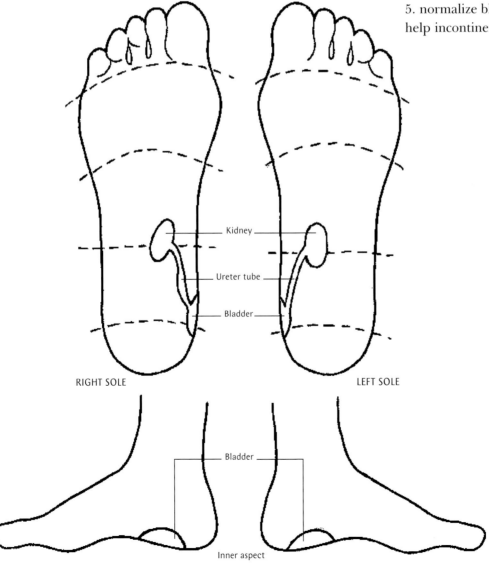

Kidney

Ureter tube

Bladder

RIGHT SOLE

LEFT SOLE

Bladder

Inner aspect

Reflexology Procedure

The Right Foot

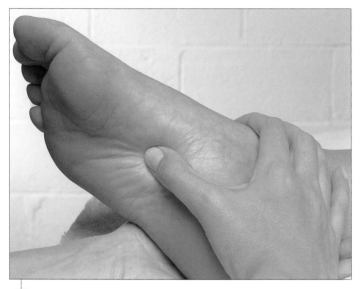

(1) Hold the right foot in your right hand, with your fingers wrapped around the top of the foot. Place your right thumb on the waist line between zones two and three and press gently into the kidney area. Circle over the area several times.

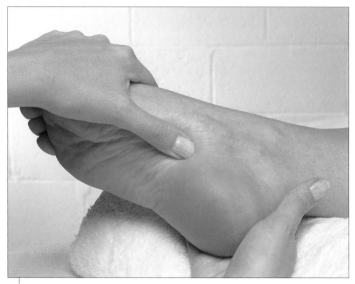

(2) Change thumbs and then caterpillar-walk down the ureter reflex toward the inside of the foot, where the bladder reflex can be found beneath the inner anklebone.

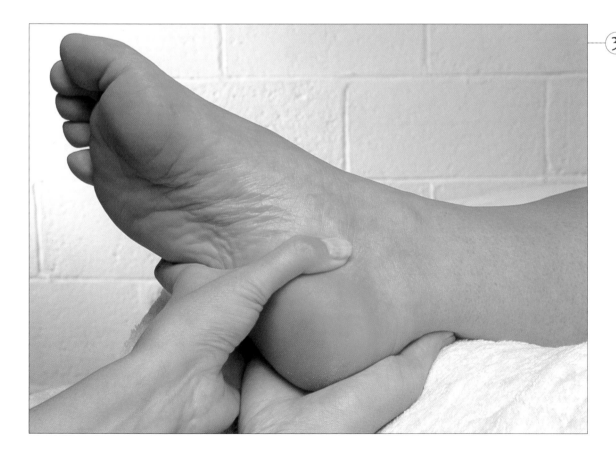

(3) Perform pressure circles or thumb-walk over this area.

CONCLUSION

I hope that by following the instructions in this book you have realized the remarkable benefits that reflexology can offer. It is such a simple, harmless, and natural way to bring balance to the body.

The increasing demand for reflexology is evidence of its enormous popularity. It used to be regarded with a great deal of skepticism and suspicion as a "way-out" therapy. But many have discovered the healing potential of reflexology, and it now plays an important role in healthcare. Students of reflexology not only include lay people, but also doctors, osteopaths, chiropractors, physiotherapists, and nurses.

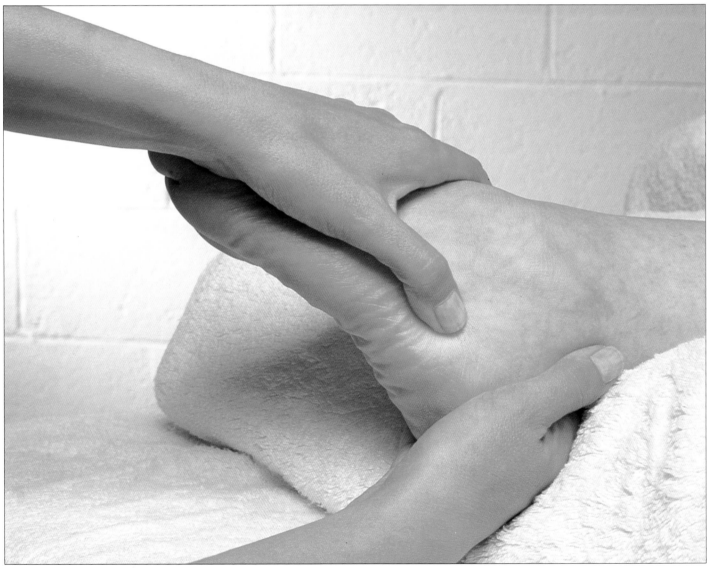

If you feel inspired by this book to learn more, contact one of the main reflexology institutes or organizations in your country. A recognized professional training will take *at least* nine months, and involves not only practical work, but also an in-depth study of anatomy and physiology, as well as the completion of many case histories.

Ensure that you check the qualifications of the principal. Is he or she a qualified teacher? How long has he or she been practicing? (At least five years is essential.) Does he or she still practice? Always ask questions, and perhaps make an appointment to view the college in action and examine the students' work.

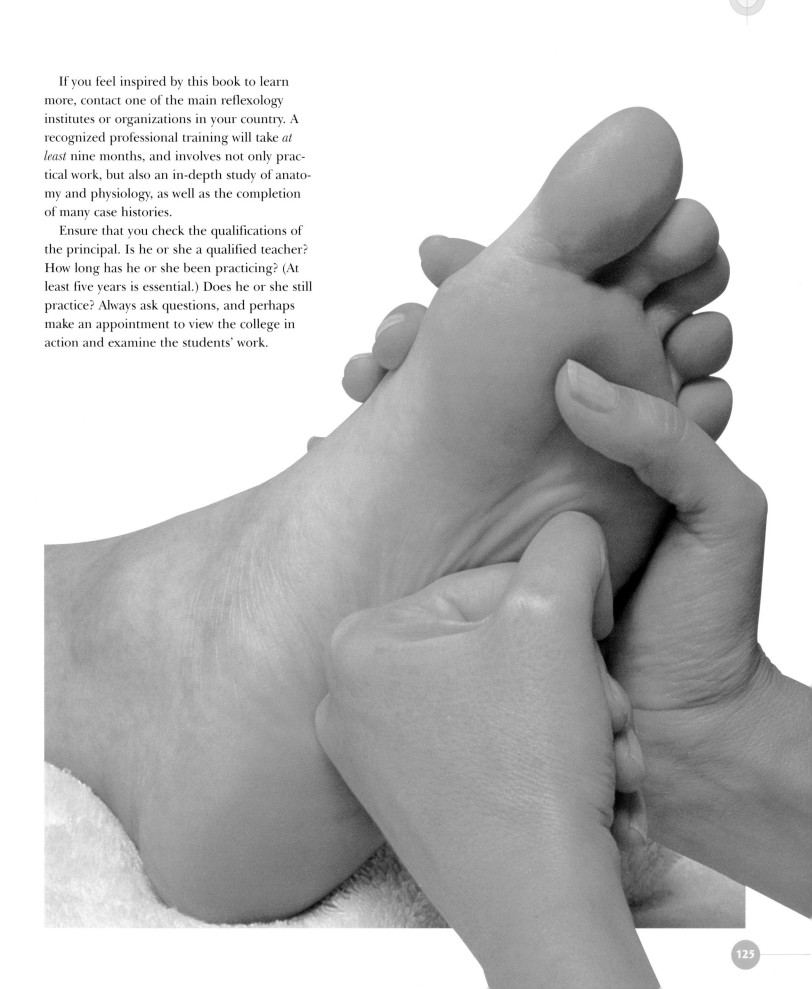

Index

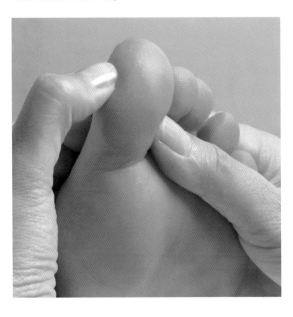

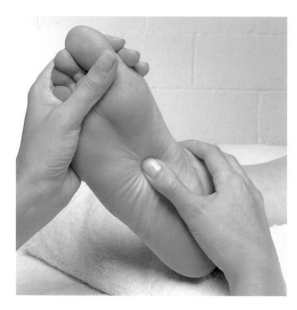

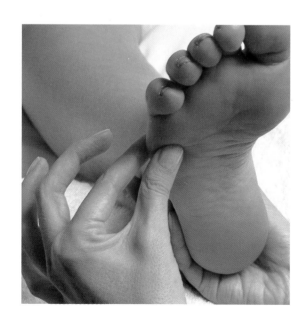

USEFUL ADDRESSES

United States

International Institute of Reflexology
P.O. Box 12642, St. Petersburg, Florida
33733–2642, U.S.A.

Reflexology Association of America
4012 S. Rainbow Boulevard, Box K585, Las
Vegas,
Nevada 89103–2059, U.S.A.

Canada

Reflexology Association of Canada (R.A.C.)
Box 110 541 Turnberry Street, Brussels,
Ontario,
N0G 1H0, Canada
Tel: (1) 519–887–9991

Credits and Acknowledgments

I would like to thank my dear husband Garry
for his painstaking efforts in deciphering my
handwriting and particularly typing and
retyping the manuscript and the diagrams.
Also for his efforts in keeping our children,
Chloe and Thomas, occupied while I was busy
with the book.

Thanks also to Sarah (and her feet!) and
Paul for their wonderful sense of humor at
the photo shoot and for making everything go
so smoothly.

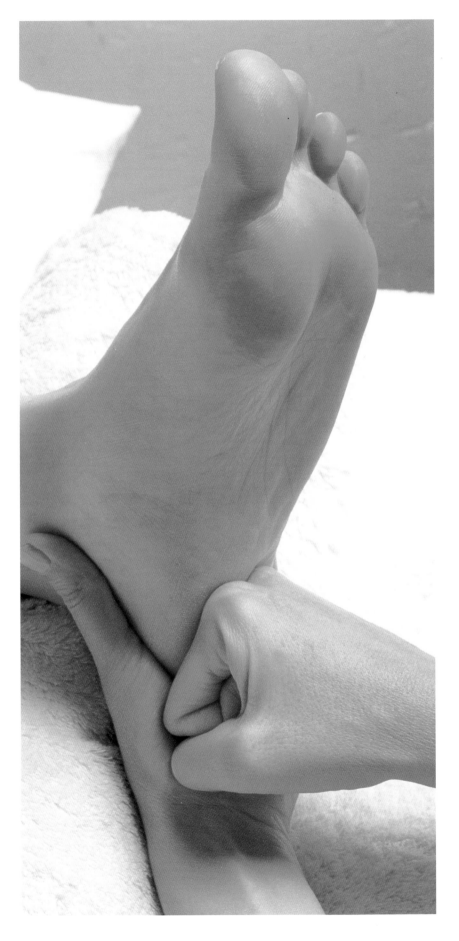